Readers Respond

TOUCHING GODLINESS

The overwhelming response of how God has touched and changed lives through the first printing of *Touching Godliness* has been a fantastic surprise. If you would like to read more of these testimonies and comments, please visit www.gfa.org.

"I have just finished *Touching Godliness*. It is life-changing and I'm recommending it to everyone I know."
—Miss P.B., Modesto, California

"Incredible book!! Never before have I read something (aside from Scripture) that has potential to be life-changing. Many books claim this distinction, but this one can deliver."
—Mr. M.W., Alton, Texas

"I now view submission as something beautiful, and beyond important in the life of any follower of Christ."
—Miss R.W., Manchester, Jamaica

"What *Revolution in World Missions* did for my view of missions, *Touching Godliness* did for my personal life."
—Mr. N.Y., Hudsonville, Michigan

"I did not read this book. My spirit DEVOURED it."
—Miss B.S., Elizabethton, Tennessee

TOUCHING
GODLINESS

"Authority exercised with humility and obedience accepted with delight are the very lines along which our spirits live."

—C.S. LEWIS[1]

TOUCHING
GODLINESS

K.P. Yohannan

BOOKS

A DIVISION OF GOSPEL FOR ASIA
WWW.GFA.ORG

ISBN: 978-1-59589-121-1

Library of Congress Control Number: 2013933840

Published by gfa books, a division of Gospel for Asia
1800 Golden Trail Court, Carrollton TX 75010 USA
Phone: (972) 300–7777
Fax: (972) 300–7778

Printed in the United States of America

For more information about other materials, visit our website: www.gfa.org.

1st printing, 2013

To

Gisela, my wife,

whose life has been,

for more than 33 years,

an example

in my own pursuit

of godliness.

And

to our children,

Daniel, Erika,

Sarah and Daniel Johnson,

for the joy of knowing

that they know the Lord and

serve Him with their lives.

CONTENTS

ACKNOWLEDGMENTS

Over the years I have learned a strange truth. There were times in which I felt I had a fresh, original revelation over certain Scriptures. Then as time went by, I would read a book written from the 18th century and there would find the author had written the same truth or revelation. Here I had thought I was the only one who had found it!

Many others went before me speaking the truths within this book to the people of God. The words from Ecclesiastes are appropriate here: "That which has been is what will be, That which is done is what will be done, And there is nothing new under the sun. Is there anything of which it may be said, 'See, this is new'? It has already been in ancient times before us" (Ecclesiastes 1:9–10).

I want to acknowledge the influence of these who have helped me in writing this book. I owe much to the writings of John Chrysostom, Andrew Murray, A.W. Tozer, Watchman Nee, C.S. Lewis, Roy Hession, Chuck Smith, Gayle Erwin and Zac Poonen. Then there are also the books and papers written on the lives of St. Francis of Assisi, St. Augustine and scores of early church fathers that gave me much understanding on the subject.

This book first started as a teaching series I did during our leaders gathering in India. Teresa Chupp, my executive secretary, oversaw this project from transcribing the 14 hours of teaching to final editing. Thank you, Teresa, for the months you spent working on this project.

Thank you, Luci, Erica, Teressa, Heidi, Kim, Tricia, Cindy and David Mains for your involvement in the project.

And to my wife and children, thank you for your prayers and help. Without your devotion to the Lord and your example, I could not have taught this series nor published this book.

INTRODUCTION

A shift seems to be taking place in the reflections of men and women on godliness and knowing God. There is a growing awareness that external things—materialism, superficial experiences, worldly success—are not what our spirits long for, nor will we ever be truly satisfied with them. Rather, our spirits hunger after spiritual realities that will not be quenched with mere "words" of correct doctrines and the "truth" without life.

The current Christianity, which for the most part is based on self, has lost its ability to influence society and be what God truly intended. Instead of living simple, devout, quiet and godly lives, like salt and light permeating society, the Church has too often turned to worldly, fleshly and carnal means to effect change.

Yet in the midst of this confusion and darkness, these brave souls are seeking for deeper healing through humility and godliness. They are discovering that an independent spirit and avoidance of pain and suffering are not the means to find that "life abundant."[1] Their spirits thirst for the living God as a deer pants for the stream. And they will not be satisfied until they drink from the fountain of living water.

There is a glimpse of "another world" in their eyes. They have seen and heard things they can't talk about. They are walking on earth, but they are not really here. There is an air about them reminiscent of the saints down through the ages like Madame Guyon, Thomas à Kempis, Saint Augustine, Saint Francis of Assisi, Watchman Nee, Sadhu Sundar Singh, A.W. Tozer and a host of others. They have touched the deep things of God and along with the psalmist testify, "Whom have I in heaven but you? And earth has nothing I desire besides you" (Psalm 73:25, NIV). There is a sense of quietness and contemplation about them. They are not moved by the opinions of others nor do they seek praise and honor from men.

Here and there you will find these who follow the Lamb gathering for feeding on God's Word and mutual encouragement. They choose to surrender their wills to God's authority. They feel the sense of unworthiness as Job did when he met God.[2] They embrace suffering and have no will of their own—the only way of truly being His.

Many look on and desire this sense of well-being and purity that comes from touching godliness. Sometimes they see it from afar. Others find it so close they can almost taste it. Yet it seems just out of their grasp. For a brief moment there may be a lingering of that spirit upon them as they encounter the reality of this godliness from those who manifest this life of Christ.

But they are not able to partake of this beauty and freshness they see in others. Their spirits long for godliness, yet their unwillingness to let go and surrender keeps the door closed, and they stand on the outside—still wishing.

We live in the day of individualism, of existential self-discovery and of fighting for liberation, where authority is seen as a servant appointed by "free men" to serve them. If authorities fail, they are replaced by a vote. The Church is full of people who have never understood the meaning of "Christ's Community," which can only happen through those who are broken and yield their wills to one another.

But as I said earlier, a new wind is blowing. The message of this book is for anyone who will join the ranks of those who seek God above all else and live with their eyes fixed on eternity.

These followers of the Lamb have a distinct mark about them: Submission.

There is a deep sense of humility and lowliness that you find about them. At home, at work, in church, in society—they manifest a quiet and gentle spirit.

Everything about their lives is marked by grace and love. If they err, they err on the side of grace, not legalism.

There is no rebellion in their attitudes. They are like their Master, the "Lamb"[3] who epitomizes surrender and submission. Their life of submission comes from the indwelling Christ, who is their life.

In 40 years of serving the Lord, I have seen and touched the beauty of Christ's life in so many, from numerous nations and various cultures. These believers manifest His likeness through their simple devotion to Him.

The *Lamb* of God has gone before us, showing the way of submission. In Revelation, we read, "The Lamb on the throne!"[4] What a paradox. The Lion of Judah made the choice to become the Lamb of God. He submitted like a meek lamb taken to the slaughterhouse, never opening His mouth. Now, however, He is sitting on the throne. The path for Him to get there was submission and obedience.

May this motto ring true of our lives: "They follow the Lamb wherever he goes" (Revelation 14:4, NIV). May we ever be His humble, gentle and broken people. If you care about the things Christ cared about and turn a deaf ear to the world—you too will begin to experience this mystery of godliness. He who has ears, let him hear.

Follow Him in life, and you will follow Him in eternity. The choice is yours. The door is open before you.

Study Guide for the Introduction begins on page 225.

ONE

The Core of Submission

*I*magine the universe without order. Our massive galaxy, the Milky Way, would spiral out of control. Our solar system, our sun and all the planets would function chaotically. There would be collisions and, eventually, utter ruin. Instead, as we look into the skies, we observe the perfect functioning of what God has fashioned.

We may have never considered it, but the reason we don't have a disordered universe today is because creation submits to the laws God established. If our moon complained, "I've been reflecting the sun's light for a long time. I choose not to submit to that arrangement anymore," it would, of course, be nothing but a dark spot in the sky.

Our wise Creator also established order and peace for mankind through authority and submission to authority. This principle transcends time and space, for even the Trinity is bound by it. God provided it for us to bring peace and a wholesome life.

In our natural world, the principle of gravity—the force that pulls us toward the center of the earth—provides us with safety and order. You can make choices in cooperation with this universal law that will enable you to live a long and healthy life. You can also choose to disregard the law of gravity and foolishly walk off of a 10-story building. But as soon as you do, you will quickly end up injured for life—or the guest of honor at your own funeral service.

Submission to authority is a thread that runs throughout every aspect of our lives. Look at your body, your hands, legs, eyes—each member must submit to the other parts of your body. When that order is violated on a cellular level, you have cancer—self-destruction.

If you go to the airport and try to get through security without submitting yourself and your baggage to the authorities, you'll end up in prison. Try to board a train without following the protocol of producing a ticket, and see what happens. The nation in which you live has established laws, and you have to obey them.

If there were no laws, no governments, no police, no submission to authorities of any kind, what would our world be like? To whatever extent you have chosen to obey and submit, it has helped you to still be alive today. Likewise, whatever tragedies have befallen the human race, the vast majority have come because of rebellion against authority.

An eagle can choose to walk around like a chicken, pecking and looking for insects, or it can submit to the laws of thermodynamics. By doing so, it can soar in the sky and enjoy the mountain peaks as few can. Yet it depends on this majestic bird choosing to submit to the laws God ordained.

To some, submission to authority always sounds negative, like somebody robbing them of their freedom. But Paul tells us that life or death is ours to choose, and in Christ, everything is "Yes," never "No."[1] Psalm 34:10 (NIV) reads, "The lions may grow weak and hungry, but those who seek the LORD lack no good thing." When we choose to obey the law of submission, we are free to live and experience life and fullness of life just as Jesus promised.[2]

The first command God gave man was to Adam. He told him that of the two trees in the middle of the garden—the tree of life and the tree of the knowledge of good and evil—he was not to eat from the tree of the knowledge of good and evil.[3] Please understand the very nature of God is love. And it was out of this love that He gave Adam and Eve the opportunity to submit to His instructions. This was for their own benefit and blessing. But Satan deceived them, and Adam and Eve disobeyed and ate the forbidden fruit.

Now we remain under a curse because we inherited the nature of Adam.[4] We are all born with a desire to resist authority and to assume that submission is our worst enemy. How quickly do toddlers just learning to speak latch onto the word "no"? Then they start using the word to defy authority. A child doesn't have to be taught to rebel! It comes quite naturally. The problem is that we are all independent and rebellious by our very nature.

Even when we become believers, our old Adamic nature doesn't just vanish. We still have to contend with it. It is through our continual choosing of the way of the cross and the work of the

Holy Spirit that we are transformed to the nature of Jesus.

This nature of Christ is one of absolute submission. Satan's nature is the exact opposite—rebellion. As we surrender to the way of the cross and choose to submit, we find freedom, healing and blessing.

IN THE POTTER'S HANDS

Do you want your life to please God? Do you desire to know His will? Do you wish to know God intimately? I'm sure you are responding, "Absolutely! I long to know God's will. Certainly I want to please Him."

Then I ask: Are you willing to give up your will and surrender unconditionally to the Lord, saying, "Your will, God, whatever it may be; that's what I want"? Maybe you're thinking, *That would be a hard prayer to pray, but in the long run, it's what I want!*

That's a good response. But then I need you to understand that your obedience to God on this matter *includes* submission to His delegated authorities, to also obey them without question, as long as they don't ask you to sin or violate the absolute authority, who is God.

Now what is your answer?

Chuck Swindoll, in his book *Strengthening Your Grip,* shares a conversation he had with General Duke about the *Apollo 16* mission to the moon. Pastor Chuck asked,

> "Once you were there [on the moon], weren't you
> free to make your own decisions and carry out some
> of your own experiments . . . you know, sort of do as
> you pleased—maybe stay a little longer if you liked?"

He smiled back, "Sure, Chuck, if we didn't want to return to earth!"

He then described the intricate plan, the exact and precise instructions, the essential discipline, the instant obedience that was needed right down to the split second. By the way, he said they had landed somewhat "heavy" when they touched down on the moon. He was referring to their fuel supply. They had plenty left. Guess how much. *One minute.* They landed with sixty seconds of fuel remaining. Talk about being exact![5]

During this mission, these astronauts obviously had to abandon their own wishes, knowing that their lives depended on it. It was definitely in their own best interests to obey. They went out on this incredible mission knowing that everything had been planned out to such precise calculations that if there were any error, it could mean their deaths.

Now consider this: We don't place our lives in the hands of human calculations, but every decision, even from our delegated authorities, is calculated and allowed by our Almighty and infallible God.

To have God's best, we must unconditionally surrender our lives to Him, which *includes* submission to our delegated authorities. This choice, however, will not come without suffering in the flesh. The old habits we have grown up with as rebellious children of Adam don't die easily. But there is one thing I am certain of: Anyone who deeply hungers to know the living God and to touch godliness will relentlessly pursue submission to God and His authority.

So submission is not something to be taken lightly. We must understand this truth in order to truly know the ways and the will of God. Look at what A.W. Tozer says: "The only thinkable relation between us [God and man] is one of full Lordship on His part and complete submission on ours. We owe Him every honor that is in our power to give Him. Our everlasting grief lies in giving Him anything less."[6]

The Lord's wish, His dream for us, is that we be our best for His glory. But He cannot accomplish this in us without our absolute submission to His will. Listen to our Father's heart in the book of Jeremiah 18:2–6 (NIV):

> "Go down to the potter's house, and there I will give you my message." So I went down to the potter's house, and I saw him working at the wheel. But the pot he was shaping from the clay was marred in his hands; so the potter formed it into another pot, shaping it as seemed best to him. Then the word of the LORD came to me: "O house of Israel, can I not do with you as this potter does?" declares the LORD. "Like clay in the hand of the potter, so are you in my hand, O house of Israel."

Let us learn to submit to this loving God even as clay submits to the potter. Only then will we see the Lord do His perfect work in and through us. God is love, and all His will is for our best. It is out of His great compassion that He established this principle and asks us to submit to His molding in our lives.

FROM ETERNITY PAST

Here we approach the throne of God as we study the foundations of a deep mystery called Authority. We are standing on holy ground; let us remove our shoes. Here our commitment must be to put aside reason as our guide. Instead, our hearts must humbly seek to learn on bended knees.

In Exodus, God told Moses His name is "I AM."[7] He is. It is from this absolute truth that Authority flows. Authority *is* God, Himself. In Isaiah, the Lord speaks of Himself, "Before me there was no God formed, neither shall there be after me. I, even I, am the LORD" (Isaiah 43:10–11, KJV).

He is the all-powerful, all-wise, all-knowing Creator and sustainer of the worlds—seen and unseen—and He is absolute Authority. He sits on His throne and reigns. There is no person and no power He reports to, and from His throne, authority flows.

Major W. Ian Thomas of Capernwray put it this way: "God is answerable to no one but to Himself, for He is the omnipotent Creator. . . . God's authority is final, and He obeys no one, for to obey would be less than an act of God."[8]

In Hebrews 1:3, the phrase "the word of His power" points toward God's creative acts being backed by His authority. At creation God spoke, "Let there be . . ."[9] And at His word, the worlds were fashioned because of the authority behind those words. Consider this statement from Watchman Nee, "In touching God's authority we touch God Himself. . . . He upholds all things by the powerful word of His authority, even as He created them by the same word."[10]

All authority on earth is delegated by God, and His appointments represent His authority. Romans 13:1 (NIV) says, "There is no authority except that which God has established. The authorities that exist have been established by God."

Why do demons leave when commanded to in Jesus' name? Because you and I are special holy people? No. It is not us, but the authority that is represented by us when we speak in Christ's name.

When you sign a letter you have written, what does it mean? It is not the words in and of themselves that make the letter valuable, but the fact that the signature represents the person who wrote them. Beyond that, it is the authority behind that signature. So when we consider the matter of authority—remember that all authority is established by God Himself. The very throne of God is established on this principle.

Submission to authority is not a man-made concept; it is instituted by the Omnipotent God. The foundation of all God's Word, even God Himself, functions on this principle.

The following verse in Romans 13:2 (NIV) says, "Consequently, he who rebels against the authority is rebelling against what God has instituted, and those who do so will bring judgment on themselves." This verse makes it clear that those who rebel against God's delegated authority rebel against God.

God will also use all His power to make certain His authority is sustained. In Exodus during the slavery of Israel in Egypt, we read about Pharaoh, one of the mightiest kings of one of the mightiest kingdoms. God had appeared to Moses and sent him to Pharaoh to release the Israelites. So Moses went to Pharaoh and said, "This is what the LORD, the God of Israel, says: 'Let my people go'" (Exodus 5:1, NIV). But Pharaoh replied, "Who is *this?*"[11]

Moses was the delegated authority, and he was representing not just words, but God Himself. So God sent plague after plague until Pharaoh was brought to his knees. This story should make us fear God. The next time we are tempted to rebel against His delegated authority, may we remember Pharaoh and choose to fear God.

Submission to authority is an eternal principle by which God Himself functions. How did Christ come to this earth? Is Christ inferior to God the Father? No. Christ is the Creator of the universe and the second person of the Trinity. His name is "Mighty God, Everlasting Father."[12] Yet we know the prophetic passage reads: "Then said I, 'Lo, I come: in the volume of the book it is written of me, I delight to do thy will, O my God: yea, thy law is within my heart' " (Psalm 40:7–8, KJV). Coming to earth was a *choice* Christ made.

In eternity past, the Trinity must have talked among themselves about the redemption of mankind. God knew all things from beginning to the end. One within the Trinity must make the decision to be the "Lamb slain from the foundation of the world" (Revelation 13:8).

Why didn't the Father come down to earth? Why wasn't the Holy Spirit sacrificed on the cross? Jesus chose: "No one takes My life from Me; I, Myself, choose to lay it down" (John 10:18, paraphrased). I can just imagine the conversation between the Father and Son before His coming to earth: "I call You Father and choose to be second. You are greater, and I submit to You. I lay aside My powers as God and will go to the earth. I will be Your servant, doing only what You tell Me, and in the end, I will go to the cross to die as a ransom for the world's redemption."[13]

What a great mystery to consider what Jesus must have done. Again, we are treading on holy ground! Logic doesn't help us here. Authority and submission are at the very heart of redemption. By this the kingdom of God is established here on earth. It is at the core of who God is.

WHO IS IN THE MIRROR— JESUS OR LUCIFER?

Unfortunately many Christians, even after decades of knowing the Lord, still remain shallow and carnal, without understanding these deeper truths of God. They have not really touched godliness. The reason is that they are still in control of "their lives" and God cannot mold them, for they are not like clay in the potter's hand. Instead, they fight to save their lives, and in the end they lose them. None of us really wants that to be true in our lives.

The following are a few questions for us to consider:

- Do you lack a sense of purpose and peace in your life?

- Is it hard for you to know God's will?

- Do you regularly experience strife and disunity with others?

- Do you feel lonely and alienated from God and your fellow man?

- Is it difficult for you to believe and obey the commands of God?

- Do you live with bitterness and anger toward those above you?

- Are you rude and unkind to your subordinates?

- Do you have careless and hurtful conversations?

- Do you live with strong unbending opinions?

- Are you quick to correct others without thinking about how you would feel if you were in their shoes?

- Do you lack humility and a gentle spirit?

- Do you lack spiritual authority when you share God's Word with others? (You may say all the right words, but God's power is missing.)

- Are you defensive when questioned about your choices?

- Do you feel hurt and offended when somebody corrects you?

- If you are in authority, do you lord it over others and cause them pain?

- Are you desperate to be in control of situations?

We have all probably experienced some of these symptoms. The reasons are many, but each of these statements indicates a certain lack of full surrender and submission to authority.

The main reason we notice these traits prevalent throughout the Body of Christ is because so many of us have not truly understood the principle of submitting to authority. Instead, we too often see believers who are independent and confused about their lives and even some whose lives end up spinning out of control.

Why is it our flesh hates submission and resists learning about it? It's because submission requires brokenness—humbling ourselves, choosing to become a lamb, not a wolf.

Christ is the picture of brokenness for us: "And while being reviled, He did not revile in return; while suffering, He uttered no threats, but kept entrusting Himself to Him who judges righteously" (1 Peter 2:23, NASB). We read in Philippians 2 that He humbled Himself to the extent of embracing death on the cross.[14] Nobody humbled Him. He chose it. There was no rebellion in Christ. He was the embodiment of submission and surrender, even though at the same time He was God.

Just as Christ manifests absolute submission and surrender, Satan manifests absolute rebellion.

Satan did not start out that way. He began as Lucifer—number one in the angelic creations. The archangels Michael and Gabriel, and all the other angels, were under Lucifer.[15] He was the mightiest and the most beautiful—the shining one.

Isaiah 14:12–15 tells why Lucifer became Satan:

> "How you are fallen from heaven, O Lucifer, son of
> the morning! How you are cut down to the ground,
> you who weakened the nations! For you have said
> in your heart: 'I will ascend into heaven, I will exalt
> my throne above the stars of God; I will also sit on
> the mount of the congregation on the farthest sides
> of the north; I will ascend above the heights of the
> clouds, I will be like the Most High.' Yet you shall
> be brought down to Sheol, to the lowest depths of
> the Pit."

How did Lucifer, this most beautiful, powerful and holy angel, become the devil? There was no sin found in Lucifer until his heart was so lifted up that he intended to set his throne above God's. This was clearly rebellion against God's authority.

Rebellion is the *seed* of Satan because it was through rebellion against authority that he *became* Satan. So sin entered the scene as a result of his insubordination and rebellion. Thus the seed of sin is rebellion. Through the sin of Adam, our lives all begin with this spirit of rebellion. But in Christ we are called out of rebellion into obedience by submitting to the authority of God.[16]

When we rebel against authority, we are not just participating in sin; we are walking into the heart of Lucifer. These are hard words. Who wants to hear them? But if we don't realize the seriousness of what we are doing, what incentive will there be for change?

This is why rebellion is taken so seriously throughout the Old Testament—so much so that rebellious children were taken out of the camp and stoned to death.[17] Read about Korah and his followers in Numbers 16.[18] Read about the kings who heard God's direction but deliberately chose their own way. Their actions left them in line for severe punishment and sometimes even sudden death.[19] When Jesus spoke with His disciples near the end of His life, He was able to say, "I will no longer talk much with you, for the ruler of this world is coming, and *he has nothing in Me*" (John 14:30, emphasis mine). During His whole life—whether it was to His earthly parents, or Caesar, or His Father in heaven—Jesus lived in submission to those who had authority over Him. There was no trace of rebellion in Him. Nothing of the ruler of this world was in Him.

May we allow the Lord to change us more and more into the likeness of Christ until there is nothing left in us from the ruler of this world.

The Way to Freedom

So God has this problem to deal with. It began in eternity past, and it will continue through to the end of time: Nothing will remain in eternity that is not of the Spirit. All that is done from self-will and independence will be rejected. Study the life of Abraham, Jacob, Moses, Joshua, Gideon and David. In all these people we find that God made sure His purposes were accomplished only through His Spirit and not through man's ability, reason or flesh.

My wife has said to me, "God must have talked to many people and asked them to do what you are now doing—people who are smarter, abler and more educated. But they didn't follow the Lord's direction. So He came to you, and you said yes."

Why did God choose me? Scripture answers that question in 1 Corinthians 1:27–29 (NIV), "But God chose the foolish things of the world to shame the wise; God chose the weak things of the world to shame the strong. He chose the lowly things of this world and the despised things—and the things that are not—to nullify the things that are, so that *no one may boast before him*" (emphasis mine).

Before Adam and Eve disobeyed and ate the fruit from the forbidden tree, they had no understanding of good and evil. This period is known as the dispensation of innocence. There was no right and wrong. All was God. And all that was done was in absolute dependence upon God. Whatever He said, that was it. They never had to reason or figure things out. Nothing in their heads was centered on themselves. They lived in absolute innocence!

Now why would God set that tree in their midst and say, "Don't eat this"? To abuse them? No!

God wanted to demonstrate to the worlds out there, to the angels, Lucifer and all the demons, that submission, surrender, is *the way* by which He accomplishes His eternal purposes. And this principle could only be validated when Adam and Eve were given the freedom to choose between submission or rebellion.

Mankind, like the angels, was given the freedom to choose to obey and submit to God's authority or to disobey and rebel. With this sacred principle, God gives us the choice to demonstrate to the seen and the unseen world that submission is the means through which His eternal purposes are accomplished.

Paul Billheimer in his classic book *Destined for the Throne* explains that the whole reason for creation was so God could find a bride for His Son.[20] Our life on earth is thus the classroom where we are trained to reign with the Lord throughout eternity. Through our choice to submit, we are being prepared to rule with Him.

God made sure that nothing in this story of redemption would have the touch of Lucifer's spirit. In Luke's Gospel, there is the story of a teenager named Mary. An angel visited her and proclaimed she would become pregnant by the Holy Spirit. Even when Mary knew she faced lifelong scorn, she responded, "I am the Lord's servant. . . . May it be to me as you have said" (Luke 1:38, NIV). In spite of all the possible consequences, she chose to *submit*.

God didn't create us to be independent. He created us to live in total dependence on Him and to have our lives in Him. When man fell, he lost his dependence on God. Now man starts out self- and flesh-centered. Satan fights to keep the flesh elevated and to cause us to depend on ourselves, not on God.

If this principle of submission to authority is so sacred, so important to God, why do we seldom hear it taught? One can be a student at a sound evangelical seminary and not be required to take a single course on submission to authority. The god of this world, as Paul said in Corinthians, has blinded the eyes of people.[21] Satan, the father of rebellion, is definitely behind our ignorance.

However, in the end God will demonstrate that the redeemed will *not* follow the spirit of Lucifer, but Him. And innocence *will* be restored. It will be all of God and none of Lucifer.

You and I are still given the choice between these two trees. We can choose the tree of life—which says, "God, You are God, and my life is in You alone." Or we can choose the tree of the knowledge of good and evil—which says, "I will find my own way with my mind, will and emotions deciding how I should live."

Jesus said,

> "Not everyone who says to Me, 'Lord, Lord,' shall enter the kingdom of heaven, but he who does the will of My Father in heaven. Many will say to Me in that day, 'Lord, Lord, have we not prophesied in Your name, cast out demons in Your name, and done many wonders in Your name?' And then I will declare to them, 'I never knew you; depart from Me, you who practice lawlessness!' " (Matthew 7:21–23).

Explained more simply, Jesus is telling these people, *You have lived your life controlled by the Lawless One, doing what the Lawless One wanted you to do.* Is it possible to be a full-time Christian worker and still be living in rebellion against God and His authority? Jesus said it was so.

Brothers and sisters, only eternity will show us how much of our work was done in the flesh without the Lordship of Christ in our lives!

This reality should grip our hearts. As I have gone through this study, I have often found myself deeply troubled and truly frightened. I also wept and asked for forgiveness. I thought about times when I was not obedient in my attitude or actions. All of us need to take these thoughts seriously and to honestly come before the Lord while on this side of eternity and let Him pour His light into our hearts.

The beginning of all new things is to let go. Let it be. Let God be God. Don't fight against Him anymore. Don't strive. I say to you: *Let it be.*

I can't explain to you the peace and rest I found in my own life when I realized that I didn't have to make anything happen! I just have to do what He tells me to do both directly and through the authority He has placed over me.

We enter into the Holy of Holies when we look into this subject, and I believe we are invited to touch a great mystery of godliness. All spiritual realities are built on this foundation of surrender and obedience. There is nothing more sacred than this truth.

May God open our understanding of this mystery of the Bride and how she is being made ready to reign with Him for eternity.

Lord, help us to fear You and surrender our lives to You. We are slow to understand. Even when we do, we often drag our feet, when we should be running after

You. Please, forgive us. Change our thinking regarding submission. Let the day be soon when we respond to this principle not just obediently but joyfully. It's a big request, but we know with Your help it can become a reality. Amen.

Study Guide for Chapter 1 begins on page 227.

TWO

THE SPIRIT OF SUBMISSION

It's all about You, Jesus,
And all this is for You,
For Your glory and Your fame.
It's not about me,
As if You should do things my way;
You alone are God,
And I surrender to Your ways. [1]

I was moved the first time I heard this contemporary worship song. These are powerful words that reflect how we should be here on earth. Our lives should be all about Jesus and for His glory. It is no longer about what we want or how we think things should be. *We* are the ones surrendering to *His* ways. This song captures the spirit of submission.

As we examine what it means to have this spirit of submission, we need to let go of our human reasoning and our cultural trappings so we can fully accept what the Word of God teaches. Unfortunately, we have inherited this rebellious nature from Adam. So don't be surprised to discover it fighting to stay alive.

We'll be helped if we allow the light of God's Word to reveal this rebellion and then deliberately choose to believe what the Scriptures say instead of what our flesh says.

After a great deal of meditation on God's Word and prayer, I have come up with the following summary of what submission to authority means:

> Biblical submission to authority is recognizing that God, my Creator,[2] is the ultimate authority[3] and has all power.[4] As clay in the potter's hand,[5] I, His creation, should yield full control of my life to His will.[6] This includes submitting to and obeying all delegated human authority over me, realizing that when I do so, I am actually submitting to God's authority. Likewise, when I rebel against delegated authority, in essence I rebel against God Himself.[7]

This definition identifies who God truly is and our place in His creation, which includes absolute obedience to Him and to His delegated authorities. I trust that this is a helpful resource as we continue our journey into understanding submission as intended by God.

THE ALPHABET FOR SUBMISSION

In all areas of life there are "building blocks." I'm referring to the components from which other things are made. For example, primary colors are the colors from which all the others are derived. The elements in the periodic table are the building blocks of matter. From the letters of the alphabet come words, sentences, paragraphs, chapters and entire books.

In this study of submission, there are also some "building blocks." The words themselves that the writers of the Bible chose are powerful stepping stones to understanding this principle. This brief study of the actual Greek and Hebrew words will be detailed, but in the end, we will be left with a picture of true submission.

Let's look first at the word usage in Romans 13:1 (NIV, emphasis mine): "Everyone must *submit* himself to the governing authorities. . . ." The Greek word used here for *submit* is *hupotasso*. It is a combination of *hupo*, meaning "under," and *tasso*, "to arrange in an orderly fashion." Putting these two pieces together, we get "to arrange under in an orderly fashion." As you might have guessed, *hupotasso* was a military term that describes soldiers lining up under their superiors according to rank.

Hupotasso here is in the present tense. It is not something a person did once in the past or will do some time in the future. Rather, it denotes constancy. It's being under submission at all times, including in the present. So it's a way of life.

In this verse, the verb form is a command. Yet even though we are commanded to *hupotasso*, the verb used here is reflexive (middle voice). This means it's the person under authority who initiates the act of submission upon themselves for their own benefit. There is no external force that makes it happen. It is a choice. Submission is not a command for us to enforce on others.

In the same verse, the word *authority* comes from the Greek *exousia,* which means "right and might." By combining all of these concepts, Paul is saying here in Romans, "Everyone must orderly arrange themselves under those who have the right and the might to rule over them."

Next let's look at Ephesians 6:1, "Children, obey your parents." Here a different term is used instead of *hupotasso.* The word *obey* in English is *hupakouo* in Greek. The meaning of *hupakouo* is "to listen to a command," and most commonly it is translated as *obey.* This is also a compound word. Again, *hupo* is "under." *Akouo* means "to listen." So putting the two ideas together, we get "listen under," which connotes conforming to a command of authority. The verb form here is also a command, but it is *not* reflexive as *hupotasso* was. It is active, which means it's the person under authority who obeys, but this action is not reflected back on them.

There is one more word I want to mention. It is the first time *submit* is used in the English Bible. This is the Hebrew word *anah.* In Genesis 16:9, Hagar, the servant of Abraham and Sarah, was running away because of mistreatment she was facing. An angel of the Lord appeared to her in the desert and spoke these words to her: "Return to your mistress, and *submit* yourself under her hand" (emphasis mine).

It is interesting to note that in dozens of other places, this Hebrew word is translated as *afflict.* The definition is "to afflict, oppress, humble or bow down." The verb form of *anah* is also reflexive, so the actual meaning in the verse becomes "to humble oneself, to be afflicted." So this angel is telling Hagar to choose to humble herself. Another way of saying this would be for Hagar to allow herself to be afflicted.

These words and their meanings are the simple alphabet for submission. Each word, and even the tenses and the patterns of the verbs, sheds light on what God wants us to comprehend about this great principle. May the Lord help us further understand His truth.

STRENGTH UNDER CONTROL

Horses are animals of great strength and beauty. If you have had a chance to watch a horse and rider at full gallop, you know it is an awesome and sometimes terrifying sight to behold. Only recently did I realize that some horses weigh as much as 2,000 pounds and can pull up to 9 tons.

I am sure you have seen or heard stories of horses that have been spooked by something. They rear up on their hind legs and kick, or they race away recklessly. It is extremely dangerous to be on the back of a horse in such a situation.

Think with me about warhorses that are found in the heat of battle. Imagine the yelling and the clashing of armies, all the sudden movements, even the animals being struck, yet they maintain themselves and aren't spooked. Neither do they run from battle. Only horses that are prepared for battle can respond in this way. Because their great strength is directed by their master, they prove a great help.

The historical meaning of the word *meekness* is "strength under control." The Greek word for *meekness* was often used to describe a wild animal that had been tamed. In many ways this meekness is precisely what we find in someone who is truly submissive. I fear that too often people link submission with weakness, which is entirely wrong. No one lies down and becomes a doormat when they submit. We don't give up the strength and ability God gave us. Instead, we allow Him to channel all this strength and ability in His way instead of our own way.

Another misunderstanding about submission is that it implies you are inferior to the one to whom you are submitting. This is also incorrect. Let's revisit the Greek words we looked at previously.

Hupakouo is the word for *obey* in the Greek New Testament. It is mostly used in cases from a superior to an inferior, like the example of children obeying their parents in Ephesians 6:1. However, *hupotasso* is also used without regard to who is the superior or inferior. For example, in Luke, after Joseph and Mary found Jesus in the temple, it says that Jesus went back with them and continued to submit (*hupotasso*) to them.[8]

When we look at the relationship between Jesus and God the Father, we know that one is not superior to the other—there is equality of the Son and the Father. Jesus said, "I and the *Father are one*" (John 10:30, NIV, emphasis mine). Yet throughout the New Testament, we are constantly reminded about His submission to the Father's authority.[9]

So the meaning of submission does not necessarily infer an inferior to a superior. Many times, as a matter of fact, whether in a marriage, in the workplace or in the government, the one under authority is stronger, abler and more intelligent. Yet this individual chooses, for the sake of God's design, to bend their knees before the throne of God.

It is easy to say, "I submit to God." But when it comes to the delegated authority over us, we can find ourselves saying, "Who is that man? He doesn't know anything. Who made him the leader? Who made him the teacher? Who made him the boss? Who made him the prime minister?" A person in charge of the local government—the chief minister, a district collector or a policeman—may be illiterate, proud, stubborn or whatever else, while you may be more intelligent, better-trained and more naturally skilled. Even so, God says, "*Hupotasso.*"

We are to submit to authority whether it is to a believer or unbeliever, someone good or bad. The appointed authority may be immoral, harsh, incompetent, even godless. The ability, character or qualifications of the authority have little to do with our submission.

All submission is a choice we make—whether to a husband, an employer, a church leader or a government official—not because of their great leadership skills, not because we are weak or inferior, but because we choose to lay down our lives and place ourselves under the protective covering God provides for us.

As I was studying the structure of submission, I confess that I found myself wondering about God's design. This was especially in regard to the concept of submitting to someone who was inferior. Then the Lord reminded me, "Who are you to question Me?" That was the end of the story.

He is the Creator. Who are we to wonder why He chose this arrangement? He alone is truly wise and good and just. Romans 9:20 says, "But indeed, O man, who are you to reply against God?

Will the thing formed say to him who formed it, 'Why have you made me like this?' " We must simply accept the design He has chosen for us.

A PICTURE OF SUBMISSION

I'm sure you have been outside when it's pouring rain. If you don't have an umbrella handy, you usually hurry toward the closest ledge or building entrance. You look for any kind of covering you can get under to protect yourself from getting all wet.

In many ways, this is a picture of what the word *hupotasso* really means. It is a deliberate action we choose to place ourselves under a covering that will protect us. It is our choice whether we will stand in the rain or take cover under what God has provided for us. No one can force us to "arrange ourselves under" our authorities. But it seems rather strange to brave the downpours on our own and end up repeatedly getting soaked to the skin.

This decision to live under the covering God has provided, however, is not just for when conditions are foul. The decision to come under this protection should be the same whether it is raining or sunny and whether or not we like a given decision made by our authority. It is a lifelong choice to deliberately and habitually bring ourselves under God's authority.

Such an act is also more than a matter of simply hearing a command and then obeying it. We are no longer on the outside, just doing what we must in order to get by. It is a choice to be on the inside. It is no longer merely external service. It is not obeying authorities for the benefits that result from good behavior. No, this is a more holy matter than a legalistic "One, two, three and done."

Submission is a matter of the heart. It is learning to think sensitively, *What does my authority really want me to do? What is he actually saying?* It is seeking to understand and then doing it.

Let's look at Elisha as an example.[10] The great prophet Elijah knew when the end of his time on earth was near. I am sure the Lord must have told him, and from Scripture, it seems his servant Elisha knew it too. Elijah wanted to release Elisha from seeing him pass from this life. Three times he told Elisha to stay back when the Lord called Elijah to another city.

Technically speaking, Elisha had every reason to say, "Yes, sir" and to stay right where he was told. But he knew his master's heart, and instead, he in essence replied, "No, I am not going to leave you! No way!" If you study the text, it is apparent that Elijah was testing Elisha's loyalty and submission to the last moments of his life. Elisha was in tune with his master's heart and obeyed his wishes instead of his words. In the end, he was rewarded with a double portion of his master's spirit.

If our hearts are truly submitted, choosing to align ourselves under the authority God has chosen for us, we too will seek to understand the heart of our authority regarding whatever matter is at hand. In contrast, if we are only seeking to obey, we will analyze exactly what our authority has said to us and figure how we can fulfill their request *and* still do what we want.

Submitting to the authority God placed over us is not like a soldier who obeys an army commander saying "Go there." The soldier may not like the command, may not believe in it and may not have any feelings about it. Yet he says to himself, *I have to fight. I am scared, but I will do it.* Submission is not like that—rather, it is much more active, pursuing, going after and seeking to do whatever the authority is thinking.

Maybe you have noticed that I have used two words here. One is *submission,* and the other is *obedience.* As I am sure you can tell, there is a difference in meaning. Submission is a heart attitude toward authority, whereas obedience is an action.

Obedience can take place through external force or requirement. In the case of submission, however, it is a deliberate choice by the subordinate to surrender to the one who is in authority over him or her.

When we submit, we will be obedient. But just because we are obedient does not mean that we have truly submitted to authority. This submission to authority is what the Lord desires in all of our lives. Even so, He always leaves us with the choice.

May we choose His way.

A Price to Pay

It is no small matter that the first time *submit* is used in the English Bible it is the Hebrew word *anah,* which actually means "afflict."[11]

It is also interesting to note that *submission (hupotasso)* is used 40 times in the New Testament. The number 40 is used in the Bible as a period of testing and trial. Think about the children of Israel who wandered in the desert for 40 years. Then it rained 40 days while Noah was in the ark, and don't forget that Jesus was tempted by Satan for 40 days in the desert. There are more stories from Scripture in which 40 represented a time of trial and wait-ing—but what does that have to do with *hupotasso?* Even in the number of times that God inspired the New Testament writers to use the word *submit,* He linked submission with trial.

At the very root of the words God used and the number of times they were used, He is communicating with us that to live in submission to Him and those He places over us is connected to trials and suffering. This suffering is not to be misunderstood as physical suffering. It says in Hebrews 5:8 (NASB) that Jesus "learned obedience from the things which He suffered." It is important to know that the kind of suffering mentioned here is not a bodily suffering, but soulish.

It will definitely hurt our Adamic flesh when we make the choice to arrange ourselves under our authority. This is one reason we find ourselves not wanting to submit—it costs inconveniences, difficulties, pain and suffering through denying of self.

As discussed earlier, we as children of Adam have the nature of rebellion. Scripture says, "The sinful mind is hostile to God. It does not submit to God's law, nor can it do so" (Romans 8:7, NIV). Without making deliberate choices against our natural way of thinking, we will not be able to experience the reality of submission. For us to submit, we must lay aside our rights, our own thoughts and our desires, which will again mean suffering. It is the act of giving in to God and saying no to yourself and your flesh.

Let's go back to Hagar and the angel's command to submit herself to Sarah. It was a deliberate decision she had to make to choose suffering in the flesh and dying to self. Hagar would have to humble herself, give in to another's wishes and allow herself to be afflicted.

Peter exhorts us in 1 Peter 2:21, "For to this you were called, because Christ also suffered for us, leaving us an example, that you should follow His steps." The suffering mentioned here is the same soulish suffering that was mentioned in Hebrews. Peter goes on further to say: "... who, when He was reviled, did not revile in return; when He suffered, He did not threaten, but committed Himself to Him who judges righteously" (1 Peter 2:23).

May we follow in His footsteps.

And All This Is for You

We should not submit simply out of fear. Neither should our actions be for the benefits that will potentially come our way. Peter tells us, "Therefore submit yourselves to every ordinance of man for the Lord's sake" (1 Peter 2:13). It is for the Lord that we ultimately submit. It is because He has asked this from us. When we submit to our authorities, we are actually submitting to the living God. It is a deeply personal response to Him.

Have you ever had someone help with a personal task or with a job related to your profession who obviously did not want to help? It's not a good experience. You'd much rather do it yourself.

God is the Creator of the universe who knew us from before the foundation of the world. He crafted time and all that it contains to bring about His best for each one of us in the midst of a fallen world. And He has given us a few guidelines to help see His best for us fulfilled. When we grumble and complain about the submission God has asked of us for our own good, should we be surprised if it would make Him sad?

Just as we love a cheerful giver, so does the Lord: "So let each one give as he purposes in his heart, not grudgingly or of necessity; for God loves a cheerful giver. And God is able to make all grace abound toward you, that you, always having all sufficiency in all things, may have an abundance for every good work" (2 Corinthians 9:7–8).

God is not as concerned about externals as He is about the condition of our heart. Submission should always be with joy, knowing we are doing this for our Lord.

Please know we won't be changed overnight. This is a process of learning and growing and becoming more sensitive. Yet when we come to that place of fully surrendering for His sake, there will be much joy.

Now we've come back full circle. The spirit of submission is choosing His way over ours for His sake.

*L*ord, You know us so well, better than we know ourselves. Shed Your light on any rebellion we still have in our hearts. We want to lay down our lives and our own wishes for You, because You are worthy. Help us, Lord, to exercise the courage to surrender and, by doing so, to fully submit to You and Your ways. Amen. ᴓ

Study Guide for Chapter 2 begins on page 230.

THREE

THE BENEFITS OF SUBMISSION

*S*ubmission to God's delegated authority is one of the most wholesome and liberating truths ever given to us by God. It affects our lives positively at every level. This truth, however, remains hidden from most of us because Satan has taken this concept and twisted it into a negative term.

Granted, submission may not be easy on our flesh, but the benefits that we receive far outweigh the struggle involved. We experience what Jesus said: "Unless a grain of wheat falls into the earth and dies, it remains alone; but if it dies, it bears much fruit" (John 12:24, NASB). When we die to our pride and submit to God's authority, the benefits *will* follow.

Before their rebellion, Adam and Eve had every blessing—all that is of God without the pollution of sin. To the extent we submit, we too will know God's restoration to that life of blessing. Likewise, to the degree we allow rebellion in our hearts, we repeat the scenes of chaos and confusion that Satan introduced into the world.

Jesus' parable of the prodigal son is a perfect picture of this truth.[1] The younger son chose to rebel and walk out from under his father's covering. He rejected the authority over him and did what he pleased. In the end, however, what he got was waste and ruin. His inheritance was squandered until nothing was left. Then famine came. The last scene of Act One has him feeding swine while going hungry himself. He lost his dignity and his honor. It was then he started thinking, *I am no longer worthy to be a son. But maybe I could ask to be one of my father's servants.*[2] He was willing to come under the authority of his father again. A.W. Tozer remarks on this story: "At bottom of his restoration was nothing more than a reestablishing of the father-son relation which had existed from his birth and had been altered temporarily by his act of sinful rebellion."[3]

When this drama ends, the son has returned. But he is not treated as a servant. Instead, he is honored as a son, with great love and celebration. Blessings are showered upon him. His father had been waiting for the day that he would return so that he could bless his son again.

We Are Protected

When we submit to authority, we are choosing to arrange ourselves under that covering that protects us.

Some years ago I went through a difficult time. Someone involved with me in the ministry, whom I loved like a brother, was deceived by some people who criticized what we were doing. He wrote a long letter to me making all kinds of accusations against me. I read his words, and it made my heart sad.

I thought to myself, *What am I going to do? Who will protect me from these charges?* I wasn't going to defend myself. Instead, I made copies of his letter and sent them to our board members. I told them, "Honestly, I don't know what to do. I cannot defend myself. Would you please look into these allegations and reply to him?"

After examining the matter, the senior board member wrote a response. I was cleared of all the accusations. It had been one of the more difficult times in my life. But God used it to teach me the importance of having authorities to protect me. There were people I could look to and say, "I need help." I was *not* all alone.

In such times, Psalm 91 is a comforting passage: "He who dwells in the shelter of the Most High will rest in the shadow of the Almighty. I will say of the LORD, 'He is my refuge and my fortress, my God, in whom I trust' " (Psalm 91:1–2, NIV). I recommend that you read this psalm in its entirety. It paints a beautiful picture for us of being under God's delegated authority and under His protection. God chooses to place people over us as an umbrella to shelter us.

Protection from the Powers of Darkness

It is the job of the shepherd to protect the sheep. Do you know what happens to a sheep that has gone astray? It is actually walking into the territory of its predators. When a pack of wolves is hunting, their instinctive goal is to go after any animal that has strayed. A wandering sheep has no shepherd to protect it, and it soon gets torn apart by ravaging wolves.

When we step out from under the covering of our authority, we become like that wandering sheep. The grass may look delightfully green on the outside of the fold, and we can sigh, "I'm tired of all these rules and regulations. I know my own way. I know what to do." But we are wandering into the territory of demons who are looking for any who have walked away from the protection of their authority.

Predators actually chase a targeted pack for the simple purpose of isolating one calf, one deer or one buffalo from the group. Likewise, one of the devil's schemes is to do this exact same thing. He will instigate rebellion against authority to draw us away from our protection. And what happens? If we are not on our guard, we will think we are justified in our thoughts and emotions and not even realize what is going on. We become independent and wander away from our covering. I've seen it happen. Although we may not realize it, when we rebel we choose to allow the demons to destroy us emotionally and physically.

I know someone who was pastoring a church, and a particular family got upset with him. They rallied a number of individuals who spread negative reports about their pastor and, in the end, tried to get him voted out of the church. Then they left the congregation in bitterness and anger along with four other families.

It was a sad situation, but not nearly as sad as the stories those five families lived out in the days and weeks and months and years that followed. Their concerned pastor watched as their lives unraveled. They stopped going to church altogether. The hearts of their children became hard and rebellious. Unexplained sickness touched various members of the families. The stories of ruin were almost too many to tell about these who once were living in hope and peace.

Their leaving the church was *not* wrong in and of itself. It was the rebellion they manifested in their hearts that brought this judgment on them.

Again, God places people over us not to hurt us, but to protect us. God told us exactly what we need to do to be free of the Enemy: "Submit yourselves, then, to God. Resist the devil, and he will flee from you" (James 4:7, NIV). We are called to submit to God, which means we are also called to submit to His delegated authorities.

You can pray all you want, you can fast all you want, you can argue all you want, you can make all the telephone calls you want, you can even go to the court of law and prove you are innocent, but the demons will not leave you alone when you are acting in rebellion. They are relentless. God is saying, "There's little I can do. I cannot get through! There's a roadblock." Its name is insubordination and rebellion. God works through His authority, through the people He sets over us. And with this covering, there is safety from the powers of darkness.

Protection from Bad Choices

Submitting to authority also gives us protection from making bad choices. It provides us with a safeguard and is like a railing so we don't go over a cliff.

In the day of the prophet Jeremiah, Jerusalem's doom was set, and the Babylonians were already on their way to lay siege against the city.[4] Even so, God provided a safeguard and a way of escape through His servant Jeremiah, a spiritual authority for Judah. Jeremiah told the people on behalf of the Lord: "Behold, I set before you the way of life and the way of death. He who remains in this city shall die by the sword, by famine, and by pestilence; but he who goes out and defects to the Chaldeans who besiege you, he shall live, and his life shall be as a prize to him" (Jeremiah 21:8–9).

The Lord sees our future, including the wrong choices we're about to make. Understanding the hearts of the Israelites, He knew they would opt to fight. Yet through their spiritual authority, He provided wisdom regarding what they should do in this tough situation.

Unfortunately, few heeded Jeremiah's godly counsel. Such is the case with all those who are stubborn and self-willed. They think they know the direction they should take, that they don't need input from others, even those God put as authorities over them. Many times, therefore, they end up making bad choices.

If we choose to submit to authority, however, it will protect us from heading in wrong directions. I know of a young man in India who is a prime example. He was blessed with godly parents who earnestly sought to teach him the ways of the Lord. Because he had all kinds of opportunities before him, there was every reason to believe he would succeed in life and become a blessing to his generation.

However, there had always been a hidden streak of stubbornness and passive rebellion in him. Though he stayed pure, his unbroken will kept him from experiencing a deeper walk with God. Then when he was in the midst of his 20s, he began to drift slowly toward thinking independently about his marriage and his future.

Finally, he ended up wanting to marry a certain young woman who was not a believer. His parents counseled him strongly against it, and he was devastated. He wept and went through deep pain. His parents suffered right along with him through his season of rebellion.

Finally, knowing his bent toward self-will, his dad told him, "Son, you can have your way; only I cannot give you my blessing. But I will not stand against you anymore."

By the mercy of God, this young man decided not to go against his parents. Through a series of incidents, he came to a place of submission. Soon after that he married a Christian girl from a godly family.

Later I asked his dad about how his boy was doing. His father said, "They are both so happy and are serving God." His son now admits how terrible it would have been had he gone against his parents' advice. This story ends well. But there are many who live with deep regrets, wishing they had listened to their parents.

Submitting to authority protects us from deception. In Jeremiah we read, "The heart is deceitful above all things, and desperately wicked" (Jeremiah 17:9). Paul also wrote in his letter to the Corinthians, "I am afraid that just as Eve was deceived by the serpent's cunning, your minds may somehow be led astray from your sincere and pure devotion to Christ" (2 Corinthians 11:3, NIV). None of us is free from the possibility of being deceived. The worst thing about being deceived is that in the midst of it, we don't realize what is happening.

Lot started his journey with his uncle Abraham, but he ended up far away in Sodom and Gomorrah. After the destruction of these cities, his family was left in ruin. He was a righteous man, yet he lost all. Why? He wouldn't seek counsel from his authority. If Lot had sought Abraham's advice about where to settle, I am sure he would not have made that terrible choice to be in Sodom and Gomorrah. Lot was deceived by the wealth and prosperity of the region, and he couldn't see where this choice would lead.[5]

In another example, Gehazi had the potential to become a prophet like Elisha, maybe even greater in his usefulness. But he became a leper and died as one. What if Gehazi had submitted to Elisha by going to him and being open about his temptation to go after the gold of Naaman? What do you think his master would have told him? To go after the money? On the contrary, Elisha would have advised him not to even think about it. That word of wisdom could have saved Gehazi from the deception that destroyed his life.[6]

When the world was offering money and position to Demas, imagine if he had come to the aged Paul and asked, "Paul, may I ask you for some advice?"

"Son, go ahead, ask!"

"You know they're offering quite a lot of money and a good position. What do you think I should do?"

I imagine Paul shaking his partially bald head and saying, "My son, it's not worth it." But Demas never sought Paul's counsel. So Paul writes, "Demas, having loved this present world, has deserted me" (2 Timothy 4:10, NASB). Because of an independent spirit, Demas made a very bad choice.

One of my senior leaders in the ministry came to me a while ago and said, "I have a personal matter I want to talk to you about." Then he explained what he was planning to do. He wanted to know what my thoughts were. So I asked him a couple of questions. From all appearances, it looked like the direction he was headed was a smart move, but I had no peace in my heart. I felt led to tell him, "I don't think this is a good move for you."

He changed his plans according to my counsel. A few months went by, and he found out some additional information about the situation. It would have been a destructive decision had he gone through with what he initially planned. It is true what Proverbs tells us: "There is a way that seems right to a man, but its end is the way of death" (Proverbs 14:12).

I have traveled many miles in my life. As I look back, I can honestly say that the decisions I made on my own, without listening to those over me, I paid for dearly. But I thank God for whatever you see in my life that is good, because it has a great deal to do with God guiding me through my spiritual authorities.

WE ARE RESTORED

Many people are living with maladies of one kind or another. I suspect if we knew the truth, we would discover that in numerous cases the trouble is rooted in rebellion. Think about the five families I mentioned who left the church. Consider the prodigal son.

But once there is repentance and people begin to submit to their authorities, the Lord starts to heal the damage of the Enemy. Wholesomeness and a clear mind are restored. When Naaman submitted to the direction of the prophet Elisha, he was actually healed of his leprosy.[7]

Look at the story of Philemon's slave Onesimus.[8] He ran away from his master and ended up in Rome. It was there he met Paul, who led him to the Lord. Onesimus became Paul's son in the faith. In a brief New Testament letter, Paul in essence writes, "Philemon, I am sending Onesimus back to you. But you know what? It's been wonderful having him with me! He's been so useful, and I have no one. He is your slave, however, so I have instructed him to return to you."[9]

Paul obviously wished that Onesimus would stay with him. But he knew the restoration and blessing of Onesimus as a new creation in Christ was connected with his willingness to return to his authority. His submission was the way he was going to grow and understand the ways of God.

Then Paul writes, "Receive him as a brother, not as a slave" (Philemon 1:16, paraphrased). Onesimus was a slave, in his own eyes and in the eyes of others. But when he actually submitted to the authority he previously ran away from, he became a brother. He was restored. How wonderful!

People who live in rebellion against authority—whether in the home, the church or a work relationship—miss out on a great blessing that could be theirs. But when they follow the submissive example of Onesimus, they know healing and peace and blessing. It will be well with them. God promises this for those who simply honor their parents.[10] Yet God not only restores us physically, He does so in a spiritual sense too.

WE LEARN BROKENNESS

Brokenness is incredibly important in our Christian walk. From a scriptural perspective, it is at the foundation of all godliness. Salvation begins with brokenness. And becoming mature in the faith is based on continuous brokenness. Galatians 2:20 is a classic verse about being filled with the Holy Spirit and becoming Christlike. Look at what it says (NIV): "I have been crucified with Christ and I no longer live, but Christ lives in me." It's about our stubborn self, which fights for its right, being broken to His will. One of the powerful tools God uses to do this is submission to those He places over us—parents, church leaders, people at work or those in government.

Submission is far more than merely obeying the authority of God and man. It is participating in the very life of Jesus. He demonstrated that all the privileges He had in heaven were far less important to Him than being in submission to His Father's authority. He submitted and chose the way of brokenness and humility.

We have fellowship with Him when we join Him and take up His yoke.[11] But to take up His yoke, we must choose to be broken and to humble ourselves. There are many who seek after godliness that still lack greatly in humility and a gentle spirit, even though they attain some degree of "righteousness of [their] own" (Philippians 3:9, NIV). They have missed this critical step of brokenness. Genuine godliness is rooted in the nature of Christ, which only comes through being a servant under His yoke.

In this age, however, we are always looking for shortcuts and easier ways. We are living in the era of microwaves. It used to take 10 minutes to boil water on the stove to make a cup of coffee. Now you open the little door, put the glass of water in, close the door, and before long, bingo, the water is boiling!

We may look at someone who is accomplished in their field and highly respected, with the title, the house, the car and all the extras. We think, *Wow! I want that!* But we forget that this person is 60 years old and went to school for many long years! It often was a prolonged journey of agony and hard work to get to where he or she is. We want all the success yet without the toil it takes to get there.

The same thing happens when we meet individuals who are especially godly. Just by being around them we feel closer to God. We admire them and think, *Wow! I want that.* We don't realize the incredible journey they walked with the Lord to get to that place. We don't see the years of faithfulness sometimes without fruit, the tears, the trials, the misunderstandings that brought them to their place of knowing the Lord and being like Him. There are no shortcuts to godliness.

Being truly pliable in God's hands is the only way we can learn to touch godliness, and God regularly uses the authorities over us to bring us to this place.

When I was a youngster, for nearly three years, I was under the leadership of someone who was often unkind to me. Our personalities just didn't mix. No matter what I did, he found fault with it. I often cried alone. Those years were one long stretch of suffering and loneliness.

Yet they were some of the best years of my life. I truly believe God was the One who placed this person over me. I knew enough at that time to realize that as long as my leader did not ask me to sin, I needed to submit. So I did. Through the combination of his harshness and my submission, I began to learn all kinds of lessons in brokenness.

Brokenness is a fruit of submitting, and submission is a fruit of being broken. You can't have one without the other. As you are increasingly submissive, it results in you being more broken. And when you are more broken, it allows you to be more submissive. Being broken means we are willing to receive correction, humble ourselves, repent for our failures and allow others to have first place. It's when we stop fighting for ourselves and become pliable in the hands of God. It is when our hearts are no longer hard but are becoming soft instead.

The Lord often uses an authority over us whom we may not like to reveal areas in which we are still hard. God led the children of Israel into the wilderness for this exact purpose: "Remember that the LORD your God led you all the way these forty years in the wilderness, to humble you and test you, to know what was in your heart, whether you would keep His commandments or not" (Deuteronomy 8:2).

Look at Jacob. God had a tremendous plan for his life. "The older shall serve the younger" (Genesis 25:23) was the prophecy. But Jacob was shrewd, crafty and independent. Actually, he was too smart. So God placed him under Laban, who was twice the crook that Jacob was, to teach him his first lessons in brokenness.[12]

Thus it is that brokenness prepares us for a greater work of God. In the book of Hosea, God speaks to the people of Israel, "Break up your fallow ground, for it is time to seek the LORD, till He comes and rains righteousness on you. You have plowed wickedness; you have reaped iniquity. You have eaten the fruit of lies, because you trusted in your own way" (Hosea 10:12–13). Before God could effectively move, their hardened hearts had to be softened.

I heard a story about a man who owned a large company. As his only son grew up, he had him do the dirty work of the factory, sweeping floors and cleaning the engine rooms. He was required to arrive exactly on time and work until the end of each day. He would come out of the factory dirty and greasy.

Years went by, and that young man grew up to be the CEO of the entire company. When the father was asked why he started his son at the bottom, he commented, "He would never have been able to handle such responsibility if I had not been willing to put him through the years of training—starting from the bottom, working his way up one step at a time. The price he paid was heavy, but now he is the owner."

In the same way, God uses submission to train us for greater usefulness. Joshua is a great example. His title was "servant of Moses."[13] How would you like to be called "servant of So-and-so"? Night or day, whatever the authority says, you are to respond, "Yes, sir." Yet Joshua became a great leader who actually stepped into the shoes of Moses! Joshua placed himself under his authority and truly lived the life of a slave, doing whatever Moses asked of him. Thus he was trained to take Moses' place when the right time came.[14]

In Isaiah 57, God tells us that He dwells with the one who is contrite and humble[15]—the one who is broken. Wow! God who dwells in heaven says He will come and dwell with me. This "dwelling with" is more than what we have in conversion.

There is a sublime power and a godliness that come through submission. It is the fragrance of the cross, of dying to oneself. It is a hundred times more potent than carnal power. Submission and brokenness are the fallowed ground that grows this kind of godliness in our lives.

BLESSED BY GOD

When we choose to submit, we have God's protection over us from the Enemy and from going in the wrong direction. The Lord restores us from the destruction the Enemy brought on our lives. We are also prepared to grow in godliness. It would seem these are benefits enough for us to choose the path of submission. But God goes beyond this and pours blessing and favor on our lives.

Think again about the prodigal son. His father not only restored him as a son, but he also heaped good things upon him.[16] God is this kind of loving Father. He's just waiting for the moment He can bless us. But all too often He is restrained by His own principles. When we live in rebellion, He can't bless us as He would like.

God's blessings for obedience and submission should come as no surprise to any of us. These thoughts are scattered throughout Scripture. The first time submission is mentioned is when Hagar is asked to go back and submit to Sarah. In the following verse the angel tells her, "I will multiply your descendants exceedingly, so that they shall not be counted for multitude" (Genesis 16:10). The book of Deuteronomy is filled with the promise of blessings for obedience and curses for disobedience.[17] Proverbs is filled with verses promising a good future for those who will take rebuke, for those who are respectful or for those who listen.[18]

We all know the story of two young women named Orpah and Ruth.[19] Their husbands and their father-in-law died. Their mother-in-law Naomi, an older woman, became their authority. Naomi decided to go back to Israel. As they were about to depart, Naomi talked to her daughters-in-law and said, "Children, I am an old woman. Even if I get married and have children, there's no way you will want to wait to have a family by them. Go back to your people."[20] Orpah wept, but she went back to Moab for security and for her future.

But we read that Ruth clung to Naomi. You have to think emotionally as you read this passage. Ruth must have reasoned this way: "My mother-in-law, she's an old woman, weak and broken. But the only person I have over me is her. Now what does she really want?" Ruth came up with her answer and then said to Naomi, "Wherever you go, I will go. . . . Your people shall be my people, and your God, my God. Where you die, I will die" (Ruth 1:16–17). In essence, she said, *Nothing will make me leave you.*

Her story of obedience continues as they return to Naomi's community. Ruth submits to all that Naomi tells her to do. The Lord then blesses Ruth, and through her He blesses Naomi. Ruth becomes the great-great-grandmother of King David and a Gentile in the line of Jesus Christ. The women of the town, in their blessing for Naomi's new grandson, say to her, "For your daughter-in-law, who loves you, who is better to you than seven sons, has borne him" (Ruth 4:15).

In the late 1960s, I was on a ministry mobile team along with about 10 others. I remember one particular morning when we were stationed near the city of Jhansi in northwest India. Our leader called me to his side and said, "You know that we are stuck."

I said, "I know." You see, our old vehicle, packed with crates of Bibles, tracts and personal belongings, had two flat tires, and we had no spares. We also had no money to buy new tires.

My leader then told me, "You are the only one who has a watch.

So why don't we sell your watch, and we can buy the needed tires?"

At first I couldn't believe he would ask me to do something like this. Though it was difficult for me to handle his request, I had been told, "Obey your leader." Honestly, it was a hard decision for me. But I prayed about it, and God said, "Obey him." So even though I didn't like it, I took my watch and gave it to him. He smiled while I cried on the inside. The watch was sold, we bought the tires, and the team went happily along its way.

I didn't remain without a watch. Actually it's amazing how many watches people have given me over the years. God has paid me back for my watch many times. One watch somebody gave me was made the same year I was born. I have also given away more watches than you can imagine. My wife says, "Your hobby is getting watches and pens, then giving them away."

Another time, when I was 20, we were in Bharuch, Gujurat, for our missions conference. During our time there, I received a letter in the mail. It was an invitation for me to fly to London and preach. They even sent me air tickets from Delhi to London and back, along with £600. I went to my senior leader, full of excitement about this invitation, and asked his permission to go. All I needed was a couple of weeks off.

He looked at me and said, "Send it back." That's all. He didn't ask me a single question about it. He didn't argue with me. He didn't even say anything except, "Send it back. You cannot go."

I just couldn't handle it. I cried and said to myself, *How can this be? It is my life. It is my invitation. How can he do this?* Then I remembered, "Obey your leader." With great pain, I sent the whole package back.

Somebody asked me recently, "Where is your home?" I replied, almost automatically, "In a suitcase." I don't know how many millions of miles I have traveled in every class on airplanes. I gave up one air ticket, one trip to England, and now I can hardly keep up with all the invitations I receive from countries everywhere to come and speak!

"Give, and it will be given to you: good measure, pressed down . . . running over" (Luke 6:38). This verse is not just about money. When we give away our rights and surrender our wills, when we give our obedience, our return is "good measure, pressed down, shaken together, and running over." I received more watches and more invitations. No angels dropped them down from heaven, but God orchestrated it. The blessings I received, I believe, have everything to do with my willingness to give up my ways and my will to submit.

Submitting to authority is never for evil, but always for blessing.

"I AM WELL PLEASED"

At the end of our lives, what could we possibly want to hear more from God than the words, "I am well pleased"? We are made by Him and for Him, and we only have this brief moment to make choices that will please our Lord. In the light of eternity, we can't even begin to comprehend how brief the 80 or so years we live on earth are. It's like it's less than a fraction of a second. Yet what we will be in eternity is determined by this split second we call time.

When we choose to say, "Lord, I will do whatever You ask me to do, no matter how difficult it is" and then are rewarded by hearing, "I am well pleased. I am happy," we have earned one of the greatest privileges a man or woman can know. I don't believe any of us is without such a desire in our hearts. When all is said and done, we want to know that we have brought pleasure to our Creator.

Scripture says our obedience pleases the Lord. "Children, obey your parents in all things, for this is well pleasing to the Lord" (Colossians 3:20). When a wife submits to her husband, God whispers, "I am pleased." Jesus said, "If you love me, you will obey what I command" (John 14:15, NIV). Meditate on the words below:

I am the Lord's! . . .
"The Lord's" to love, to honor and obey.
I am the Lord's! Yet teach me all it meaneth,
All it involves of love and loyalty,
Of holy service, absolute surrender,
And unreserved obedience unto Thee.[21]

These are the words of a hymn written by Lucy Ann Bennett at the turn of the 19th century. Our love and our devotion are intertwined with our obedience to Him, which also means to His delegated authorities. To love the Lord is to obey Him and His delegated authorities, His covering over us. There are few greater ways to express our love to Him than to surrender our wills to His.

Jesus Christ, Creator of the earth, moon, sun, stars and all the galaxies, came to earth as an infant. He emptied Himself and walked on this planet like us. During the first 30 years of Jesus' life, we never hear God the Father say "I am well pleased" about

His Son. But when Almighty God, now a man, chose to walk down into the water and bend His neck under the hand of a man whom He created and submit Himself to go under the water, the voice came from heaven: "This is My beloved Son, in whom I am well pleased" (Matthew 3:17).

"I am well pleased." May it ever ring in our hearts.

*L*ord, we bow our hearts before You. You alone are God. You alone are wise. Yet too often we find ourselves thinking we know better. Lord, in Your grace, remind us that You put authorities over us for our protection, and that as we submit to them, we become more like You and experience Your blessing in our lives. Thank You for all the benefits You grant us through submission. Help us, Lord, to choose this path for You. Amen.

Study Guide for Chapter 3 begins on page 232.

FOUR

CHRIST, OUR EXAMPLE

The title "the Lamb" . . . describes His character. He is the Lamb in that He is meek and lowly in heart, gentle and unresisting, and all the time surrendering His own will to the Father's. . . . Anyone but the Lamb would have resented and resisted the treatment men gave Him. But He, in obedience to the Father and out of love for us, did neither. . . . No standing up for His rights, no hitting back, no resentment, no complaining! . . . When the Father's will and the malice of men pointed to dark Calvary, the Lamb meekly bowed His head in willingness for that too.[1]

This is our Lord. As portrayed by Roy Hession in the above quote, even Jesus' title of "Lamb of God"[2] symbolizes submission. His life on earth is a perfect example of submission to authority. As believers, it is not a set of laws we follow; rather, it's the person the Lord Jesus Himself.

The human race fell through the first man Adam's disobedience. Redemption came through the last Adam's obedience.[3] To demonstrate this truth to the *worlds,* the Trinity chose to bring redemption through obedience.

Although Jesus is equal to the Father and the Holy Spirit in the holy Trinity, by His own choice, He "became flesh and dwelt among us."[4] Thus, He is our "forerunner,"[5] the One who showed us the way we must live.

But Christ can only be an example for us if He had no advantages over us. If you believe Jesus was a super-angel walking around, you are mistaken. Though He was God, He "emptied Himself" of His divine privileges and became man.[6] He was tempted in every way that we are and had all the emotions we have. Yet He was always victorious, but only by the same means that are also available to us.[7]

In the book of Revelation, Jesus confronts the church in Laodicea with their failure to overcome the temptations they were facing. Jesus told them, "To him who overcomes, I will give the right to sit with me on my throne, *just as I overcame* and sat down with my Father on his throne" (Revelation 3:21, NIV, emphasis mine). He is essentially saying, "I understand. You are not the only ones who have faced an onslaught of temptations. I remember encountering the exact struggles that are facing you— *but* I did not give in." And He exhorts them, "Just as I overcame, you can overcome."

That is what our Lord is telling us today: "Just as I overcame, you too can overcome." He invites us to use His life as the model. Let us follow His example of submission to authority.

LEARN FROM ME

While the Old Covenant is all about rules, regulations and obedience to laws, the New Covenant is God's invitation for us to be "partakers of the divine nature."[8] Through the life and death of Christ, we are restored to God's eternal purpose for man—to manifest His nature.[9] His death was the means for our redemption, but by His life as a man, He showed us how God intends for us to live. John says of Jesus, "In Him was life, and the life was the light of men" (John 1:4). His life—His character and His example—is the "light of men."

This does not mean we just imitate Christ. Many people, such as Mahatma Gandhiji, imitated Christ.

It is not to be like those who join the army. They come in with long bushy hair and their own look. But soon, they end up in the barber's chair, and their long curly hair is gone. Their fancy civilian clothes are replaced with an army uniform, and all the soldiers now look the same. As long as they are in the army, they will behave as they are told. They are just copying behaviors. On the inside, however, they may still be something else.

As followers of Christ, we cannot copy behavior, imitate and therefore become godly. Godliness, becoming like Christ, is not an objective list of rules. In fact, a purely intellectual knowledge of Christ will leave us proud and self-centered still. Rather, godliness is born out of a growing and alive relationship with our Lord. Hence, we read in John 15:4, "Abide in Me, and I in you." In Ephesians, the phrase "in Him" is repeated again and again.[10] Our life only makes sense when we understand that our very identity and source of life come from Christ. We are not on the outside. We are on the inside. It is no longer our life, but Christ's life manifesting itself in us and through us.

"Come to Me" and "learn from Me," Jesus told His disciples. But there is a condition: "Take My yoke upon you."[11] You cannot learn of Him unless you take His yoke. What does His yoke represent? When I was growing up in my village, there were paddy fields everywhere. To plow these fields, farmers used a set of buffaloes with a yoke placed over their necks. The rear of the animals had several burn marks on them, like stripes. I remember as a youngster asking a man, "Why do all of these animals have burn marks?" He said, "It is the sign that they are broken and submissive."

When Jesus said, "Take My yoke," it means He had a yoke. He was broken and submissive. Now He invites us to come under that yoke of submission next to Him, choosing to give up what "*I want*," even in good and right matters, for His will.

Once we are willing to do that, we begin to manifest the nature of Jesus. A.W. Tozer says it this way, "If we cooperate with Him in loving obedience, God will manifest Himself to us, and that manifestation will be the difference between a nominal Christian life and a life radiant with the light of His face."[12] In the measure by which we open our life to Christ and bend our necks to the yoke, dying daily to our self-centeredness, independence, pride and reasoning, and instead depend on God, in the same measure we will manifest His nature in our lives.

Our self-will, our way, our wish, what we want is the enemy of submission and brokenness. Make no mistake: When we say no to self and yes to God, we will suffer in the flesh. The Bible says Jesus learned obedience through *suffering*.[13] Throughout His lifetime, from the day He was born to the last minutes before He died, He suffered in the flesh, saying *no* to what He wanted and *yes* to the Father's will.

When an authority asks us to do something that seems unjust, it is easy for us to become defensive and angry and, if we are not careful, say things we will regret, whether to them or others. What did Christ do? He said, "I accept the suffering. This is from Your hand, Father. I am happy to suffer for You." When His earthly parents, the creation of His hands, were scolding Him or behaving in ungodly ways themselves, God was living in their house and looking at them, watching and suffering on the inside—but without bitterness, anger or condemnation. He didn't correct them or abuse them; He just suffered.

In His flesh, He died daily. And He left His example that we may understand this principle. But unless we embrace it, we may imitate godliness, but we will never actually *become* godly.

FOR I AM GENTLE

Sin is a manifestation of the independent spirit of pride and self. In Christ there was no sin. There was never a moment in His life of worry, fear, strife, bitterness, unforgiveness or pride. After Jesus told His disciples "Learn from Me," He continued, "for I am gentle and lowly in heart" (Matthew 11:29). There was no trace of self-promotion, disobedience or rebellion in Him.

He then closed His sentence with, "and you will find rest for your souls."[14] When we die to pride and self, there is rest from worry, fear, unforgiveness and all the manifestations of our flesh. We come to a place of peace saying, "Lord, whatever You want." Madame Guyon said, "[When you are so sustained by God] a new kind of peace will come to you. . . . It is the kind of peace that a dead man would feel in the middle of a great storm at sea. . . . Deep below it is tranquil. The outward senses may suffer pain, but the deepest parts of the spirit dwell in undisturbed rest."[15]

Just before He went to the cross, Jesus said to His disciples, "My peace I give to you" (John 14:27). Think about it: In the final hours before His death by crucifixion, when the sins of all humanity would be set upon His shoulders, He was able to essentially say, "My peace, the peace that is mine right now, I give to you." These words transcend human understanding.

The key to Christ's life on earth—all that happened in Him, through Him, by Him and for Him—was due to His submission to His Father. This also meant submitting to the delegated authorities over Him while He lived on earth.

Those who follow Jesus will also have this same mark of submission on their lives.

ONE STEP AT A TIME

Consider this: Christ started His public ministry at the age of 30. Why did He have to wait until then? On top of that, why was there another three-and-a-half years before the cross? Couldn't He have started His ministry when He was 18?

When I was a boy, my mother took me to kindergarten. There were about 30 lads like me who sat in a circle with our guru (teacher), who taught the alphabet to us in our native language. Each year I passed on to the next grade and eventually on to high school and college.

A primary-school student learns subtraction and multiplication, but the college student deals with calculus. In the lower grades, a child draws pictures or writes papers on simple subjects. But at a university, the scholar reads a 2,000-page book and writes a 10-page paper. It's a whole different world.

So why did Christ have to wait 33 years before He went to the cross? For Christ *the man* to choose absolute surrender to the point of death on the cross, He needed time to grow in obedience. The Bible actually says that Jesus *learned* obedience.[16]

When His parents made mistakes and Jesus suffered, instead of sinning against them, He grew in obedience. Like this, He learned obedience through the years until He came to the place at which He was ready to lay down His life.

So it is in our own lives. God does not start us out with calculus and a 10-page paper. We can trust that the opportunities He gives to us to learn obedience—whether to Him directly or to a delegated authority—are at our current level of growth.

As we submit in our hearts, step by step the Lord will bring us to a place where we hold nothing back from Him. Paul encourages us, saying, "He humbled Himself by *becoming* obedient to the point of death" (Philippians 2:8, NASB, emphasis mine).

His Journey

"For we do not have a High Priest who cannot sympathize with our weaknesses, but was in all points tempted as we are, yet without sin" (Hebrews 4:15). As a human being, Jesus faced the same temptations we do, even in this difficult area of submission to authority. He too must have been tempted at times to disobey authority and not show them honor. Yet He was without sin.

Jesus was 12 when His parents found Him learning in the temple with the teachers.[17] He was about His Father's business. When confronted by His parents, He could have chosen to rebel and say it was more important for Him to stay in the temple. But He chose instead to submit to His heavenly Father's will by submitting to His earthly parents: "Then He went down with them and came to Nazareth, and was subject to them" (Luke 2:51).

From Luke 2:24 we can deduce that Joseph and Mary were not well-off. They sacrificed two pigeons or turtledoves, which was the Lord's instructions to those who could not afford a lamb.[18] According to Mark 6:3, Jesus had at least four brothers and two sisters at home. That means there were at least nine members of the family.

Living in cramped quarters and not always having enough money, there was plenty of room for irritation. John 7:5 says that His brothers did not believe in Him. You can imagine the sibling rivalry when there was an older brother whose place in the family was held in question.

Yet in this complex family situation, with all the misunderstandings, missed judgments and scoldings that must have happened, Jesus continued to submit to the authority that was over Him. It would have been easy for Him to just walk away from it all. But He didn't.

While Christ was on earth, at any time He could have returned to heaven and resumed the throne and His rule as part of the Godhead. He never ceased being God. He only laid aside His powers. It was a choice He made to submit Himself to the Father and live in total obedience. In John's Gospel, He says, "I lay down My life that I may take it again. No one takes it from Me, but I lay it down of Myself. I have power to lay it down, and I have power to take it again" (John 10:17–18).

Jesus could have said, "I'm stopping this whole thing and going back to heaven. I can't continue to live under these people and their decisions." We sometimes respond that way to delegated authority, but Christ didn't. Instead, for 30 years He lived in subjection to the human authority of His imperfect parents.

Luke 2:52 reads, "And Jesus increased in wisdom and stature, and in favor with God and men." I have no doubt that His increase in wisdom and favor with God and men had everything to do with His choice to submit to their delegated authority.

Joseph was a carpenter and so was Jesus.[19] According to custom, Jesus would have learned this trade from His father. As He never sinned, Jesus must have faithfully submitted to Joseph's instructions about being a good carpenter and taking care of the family business.

Throughout the Gospel of John, we read of Jesus making statements like, "I do nothing of Myself,"[20] "I say whatever the Father tells me to say"[21] and "I do exactly as the Father commanded Me."[22]

We all know Jesus is the One who called His disciples. But toward the end of His life on earth, He says to the Father, "I pray for them . . . for those whom You have given Me" (John 17:9). How do we explain that? Nowhere in the Gospels do we find the Father calling these men to Christ.

Let's look at what happened the night before Christ called those men. He spent all night in prayer seeking the Father, and by morning, He knew exactly whom He must choose.[23] Jesus did not pick the disciples Himself but did exactly what the Father told Him.

Minute by minute He did what His Father instructed Him to do. Obviously there were many times when this meant that Jesus the man had to say no to what He thought and yes to the Father. But He chose to obey His Father and suffered in the flesh.

One of those many times is found in John 11. Christ did not have very many friends.[24] But there was one family we hear of numerous times—Lazarus, Martha and Mary.[25] He loved them very much.[26] In the midst of all the busyness of His schedule, He was able to find rest at their home in Bethany.

Then one day, Lazarus's sisters sent word to Jesus: "Lord, the one you love is sick" (John 11:3, NIV). Notice the message wasn't, "Lord, please come! Lazarus is sick and is dying!" It's nothing like that, just this one statement: "The one you love is sick." The Gospels are filled with people pleading, but it's not that way here.

Why was that? It was common knowledge that Christ deeply loved Lazarus and his sisters. They fully expected that the moment Christ heard Lazarus was sick, He would drop everything and rush to see him. In Bethany they waited for Jesus for days, and He didn't come. So they sat beside the bed and watched Lazarus die. He was buried, days went by, and still Jesus didn't come.

When they said to Jesus, "The one you love is sick," our Lord did not go but stayed in the same place for two days. You see, each moment He lived under obedience and submission. He must have said, "Father, Lazarus needs Me; what should I do? Am I to go and heal him?" But the Father said, "Son, don't go. Wait."

As a man, Jesus obviously would have wanted badly to go to Lazarus. He was moved to weeping and groaning when confronted with Lazarus's death. Yet when He heard the Father's response, He must have answered saying, "I accept the suffering, Father. If that is what You say, I will wait."

Christ's life was always marked by absolute obedience and submission to His Father. But please don't misunderstand—Christ was not a weak person by any means. He was a leader in every sense of the word. People were amazed at the authority with which He spoke.[27] He commanded demons to flee, rebuked the wind and sea, and even called Lazarus to rise to life from his tomb.[28]

His authority came out of His submission to His Father. He said, "For I have not spoken on My own authority; but the Father who sent Me gave Me a command, what I should say and what I should speak" (John 12:49). Let me remind you again: We cannot say we submit to God and at the same time, on the inside, live a life of insubordination and rebellion toward the authority God has placed over us. Watchman Nee says, "Submission to God is not possible if we are not in submission to those He has placed over us."[29] Our submission to God is a reflection of our submission to our delegated authority. In the same way, our submission to our delegated authority is a reflection of our submission to God.

Jesus also submitted to the government of Rome, and He encouraged others to do so. His enemies tried to trap Him in His words, asking, "Is it lawful to pay taxes to Caesar, or not?" (Mark 12:14). This was a controversial issue of that day. God's chosen people were governed by a foreign power. There were Jewish rebels in Jesus' day who encouraged the people not to pay taxes lest they come under man's rule instead of God's. Jews begrudged paying taxes to the Romans, and some even considered it treason.

Jesus answered their question, "Render to Caesar the things that are Caesar's, and to God the things that are God's" (Mark 12:17). He told them that despite being under another nation, they were to submit to the government over them.

Jesus submitted to Pilate during His trial and at His sentencing. Jesus knew the decisions made by Pilate were ultimately directed by God. He told him, "You could have no power at all against Me unless it had been given you from above" (John 19:11).

When He was arrested the night before, He was able to say, "Shall I not drink the cup which My Father has given Me?" (John 18:11). He knew it was not from the Pharisees, the Roman soldiers, the Jewish people or Judas. He could say, "No, it's from My Father, and I submit to Him."

Even earlier that night, in the Garden of Gethsemane, Jesus had prayed, "Father, if it is possible, may this cup [the cross] be taken from me. Yet not as I will, but as you will" (Matthew 26:39, NIV). At a glance, it would seem that Jesus appeared frightened by what was about to happen, including the horrible death He must suffer on the cross, and so was looking for a last-minute way of escape, wishing salvation could somehow be achieved by another means.

But what did He actually mean? Watchman Nee explains:

> It is the highest prayer in which our Lord expresses His obedience to God's authority. Our Lord obeys God's authority first, more than sacrificing Himself on the cross. He prays earnestly that He may know what is the will of God. He does not say, "I want to be crucified, I must drink the cup." He merely insists on obeying. He says in

effect, "If it be possible for me not to go to the cross," but even here He has not His own will. Immediately He continues with, "but Thy will be done."[30]

The cross and sacrifice were not Christ's focus, but rather the will of God. Death on the cross was not an absolute to Christ; the Father's will was the absolute.

More than a thousand years earlier, King Saul had told the prophet Samuel, "But the people took . . . the best of the things which should have been utterly destroyed, to sacrifice to the LORD your God" (1 Samuel 15:21). Saul must have thought to himself, *I want to sacrifice to God who gave me this victory. This is wonderful.*

But Samuel told him, "Has the LORD as great delight in burnt offerings and sacrifices, as in obeying the voice of the LORD? Behold, to obey is better than sacrifice, and to heed than the fat of rams" (1 Samuel 15:22). Saul had been handpicked and anointed by God, but because of his disobedience, God rejected him, regardless of the sacrifice he was prepared to make.

Even in the last minutes of His time on earth, Christ's sacrifice on the cross was secondary to His greater concern—submitting to the will of God.

AS FOLLOWERS OF CHRIST

I pray that God will open our eyes to understand His ways. I write these words not as someone who has learned these lessons, but as a person who has a long way to go. I am concerned for us as the Body of Christ. I know many who follow the Lord and work hard, sacrifice much and go to the ends of the world. But the question remains for all of us: Is it out of pride and self-assertion?

Or is it done out of obedience to God in the brokenness and submission of Christ?

Hopefully none of us from the perspective of eternity will look back with regret to see much done "for God" because we were smart, had the ability, had the money and the title—but in the end we were actually disobedient to God's purposes. We did not listen to the authority God placed over us; we did not listen to God. We did many things "for Him" but without the brokenness and submission of Christ.

My hope is that someday we will have a community of Christ raised up that understands what it means to walk in submission like our Lord did, living in submission to God and His authorities.

Roy Hession continues his words about Jesus, the Lamb of God:

> It was as the Lamb that Isaiah saw Him, when he prophesied, "He is brought as a lamb to the slaughter, and as a sheep before her shearers is dumb, so he openeth not his mouth." The scourging, the scoffing, the spitting, the hair plucked off from His cheeks, the weary last march up the Hill, the nailing and the lifting up, the piercing of His side and the flowing of His blood—none of these things would ever have been, had He not been the Lamb.[31]

The Moravian Church that sought the Lord so fervently in the 18th century displays these words on their emblem: *Our Lamb has conquered. Let us follow Him.* May that be our commitment.

How painful it is for us, O Lord, to be confronted with our nature of rebellion. Thank You so much for the example You set for us, for showing us the way. Help us to hunger after You. May we too learn the godliness that comes through submission. Thank You for Your grace. We know it is sufficient. Amen.

Study Guide for Chapter 4 begins on page 235.

FIVE

WE MUST OBEY
DELEGATED AUTHORITY

*I*magine you are in rush-hour traffic in Bombay, India—one of the world's most crowded cities with more than 18 million people. Streets are jammed. It's like a swarm of ants—buses, trucks, cars, auto rickshaws, bicycles and pedestrians everywhere. I've heard it said, "Our traffic system in India is the most organized confusion in the world." And this is what you're looking at—this organized confusion.

In the center of this maze stands a skinny little man. Now you're thinking, *Does he want to get himself killed? What in the world is he doing in the middle of all this hubbub?* But there is more to the picture. This is not just anybody—this man is dressed in a tan uniform, with the hat and badge of a traffic policeman, holding a sign that reads "STOP."

Mind you, he's no celebrity or public figure. He may have never been to college, but the moment he holds up his sign, you can hear the screeching of brakes. All the vehicles stop—Mercedes-Benzes, taxis, BMWs, trucks, you name it. It makes no difference whether the people in the vehicles are politicians, truck drivers, movie stars or taxi drivers, Sardarjis, Malayalees, Oriyas, Europeans or Americans. Everybody comes to a halt. When the man in the uniform waves them on, off they go once again.

Let's say the following week this same individual comes to the same spot, but he's wearing his *pajama kurta*[1] while standing in the middle of this crazy Bombay intersection. Now what do you think is going to happen? "Oh!" you say. "This time he will get killed!"

What's the difference? When he stands there as an officer, he's *not* just representing himself. His uniform, badge, cap—they all indicate he works for a higher authority. He represents the laws of the land, the judges and the punishment that awaits those who disobey. If you choose not to follow his directions, you will have more than just him to deal with. As a policeman, he has the backing of his superiors' power. He is not the authority himself. He simply represents it.

In the same way, *our* delegated authorities represent God. When you rebel, you are not simply disobeying your husband— you are disobeying the Lord. When you whisper criticism about your pastor, you dishonor God. When you take your employer lightly, you disregard the authority with which God backs him.

Look at Romans 13:1–2: "The authorities that exist are appointed by God. Therefore whoever resists the authority resists the ordinance of God." The word *ordinance* means something specifically ordered or ordained. It's an official decree, and in this case, a decree ordered by God. With absolute understanding of His purpose for time and eternity, the Lord places people in authority. For us to reject that authority is to reject God Himself.[2]

Throughout Scripture, we see this principle clearly illustrated. When the children of Israel wanted to be like other nations and have a king instead of Samuel, Samuel thought the Israelites didn't want him. But God explained, "They have not rejected you, but they have rejected Me" (1 Samuel 8:7, NKJV).

The same is true today. When we reject the authority over us, we are actually opposing God Himself.[3] I don't know how you feel about this, but it causes me to have a holy fear regarding delegated authority.

When you speak privately against your boss at home or on the phone, when you criticize authority, whether it is the prime minister, the president or a cabinet member, God responds in the same way: "They have not rejected their human authority; they have rejected Me."[4] This thought should cause us to be sober.

If we truly realized that the authorities—in our nation, at work, in the church and in our homes—are actually God's delegates and not just the people we see or read about every day, we would have less difficulty obeying them. If we could picture them as that policeman in the Bombay intersection—with a uniform and badge indicating they represent the authority of the living God—it would change everything for us.

ESTABLISHED BY GOD

When God appoints someone as His representative, He stands by them. Numbers 30 is a serious passage. An Old Testament law stated that if a woman made a vow, it was only binding if her father said nothing against it. If she was married, her vow had to be approved by her husband.⁵ God would rather have her obey authority than maintain her vow. He would not hold her responsible because her delegated authority was over her. Not even God will supersede delegated authority.

In fact, God uses His power to establish His authority. This includes warnings, correction, discipline and setbacks. The continuation of Romans 13:2 says, "Those who resist will bring judgment on themselves." Punishment awaits those who rebel against delegated authority.

Remember Miriam?⁶ When Moses was born, he was put in a basket and placed in the Nile to keep him from being killed. And who helped? Miriam, his older sister. But as an adult, even though he was the younger brother of Miriam and Aaron, Moses was still their God-appointed authority. It was their responsibility to respect him and obey him as God's representative.

But "Miriam and Aaron began to talk against Moses because of his Cushite wife, for he had married a Cushite. 'Has the LORD spoken only through Moses?' they asked. 'Hasn't he also spoken through us?' " Next we read, "And the LORD heard this" (Numbers 12:1–2, NIV).

God called to them, "Come out."⁷

I imagine Aaron and Miriam looking at each other and saying, "Good! God wants to talk to us! What we are saying must make sense to Him too."

But the story turns out differently. Instead God says, "Listen to my words: When a prophet of the LORD is among you, I reveal myself to him in visions, I speak to him in dreams. But this is not true of my servant Moses; he is faithful in all my house. With him I speak face to face, clearly and not in riddles; he sees the form of the LORD. Why then were you not afraid to speak against my servant Moses?" (Numbers 12:6–8, NIV).

You see, when the living God appointed their younger brother to a place of authority, it was no small matter. Therefore, judgment came upon Miriam for her disrespect, and she was immediately afflicted with leprosy.[8]

Aaron then asked Moses to intercede for her healing, pleading, "Please, my lord, do not hold against us the sin we have so foolishly committed" (Numbers 12:11, NIV).

So Moses prayed for her, and the gracious but stern response of the Lord was, "If her father had spit in her face, would she not have been in disgrace for seven days? Confine her outside the camp for seven days; after that she can be brought back" (Numbers 12:14, NIV).

How many people today walk around with a similar leprosy, only on the inside? They can't sleep, and they no longer have a glow about them. They are bruised and hurting. I have been in this place in my own life. You know, brothers and sisters, the sooner we learn to submit and respect authority, the better it will be for us.

The story of Korah in the Old Testament is one of the most sobering accounts you can find.[9] Being a Levite, Korah was called by the Lord to serve His people. He was a person who represented supremacy in spiritual matters. He and his friends, Dathan and Abiram, rallied 250 *leaders*—not a couple of little boys, but 250 *leaders*—to rebel against Moses and Aaron.

They gathered together in their opposition and said to Moses, "You have gone too far! The whole community is holy, every one of them, and the LORD is with them. Why then do you set yourselves above the LORD's assembly?" (Numbers 16:3, NIV).

Moses immediately fell facedown and proposed to let the Lord choose who should come near Him. Then he added, "Isn't it enough for you that the God of Israel has separated you from the rest of the Israelite community and brought you near himself to do the work at the LORD's tabernacle and to stand before the community and minister to them? . . . It is against the LORD that you and all your followers have banded together" (Numbers 16:9, 11, NIV).

The next day, along with Moses and Aaron, this large group was to come bearing incense and fire before the Lord, to see whom He would choose. I'm sure Korah's large company had little doubt that they were right and would be proven so. They thought they were simply opposing Moses and Aaron. They never imagined they were defying God Himself, for they pictured themselves as His people. I'm sure they fully intended to keep serving *Him*.

Do you remember how severe their judgment was? God said, "Moses, step aside. I am going to wipe out the whole congregation."[10] But Moses pleaded with the Lord to show mercy. So God said, "Alright. Tell everyone to move away from the tents of Korah, Dathan and Abiram."[11]

Next we read these chilling words: "And the earth opened its mouth and swallowed them up, with their households and all the men with Korah, with all their goods. So they and all those with them went down alive into the pit; the earth closed over them, and they perished from among the assembly" (Numbers 16:32–33).

How many people perished? How many children and old people died? And for what? For rebelling against delegated authority. God will stand by those He has appointed to represent Him!

Aaron had already learned the hard way the price of rebellion. In the book of Leviticus we find the story of his two sons, Nadab and Abihu.[12] Ten times their names are mentioned alongside their father the priest.[13]

His sons helped with the offerings and the sacrifices. What a holy job! But something unfortunate happened. They decided to offer fire before the Lord themselves, bypassing the authority of not only their father, but also a priest.

Yesterday, the day before, all last week and last month, they saw their father performing his ministry before the Lord. They were right there with him as his assistants, and they got used to what was going on.

Aaron would say, "Give me the fire."

"Yes, Dad. Here it is." And they'd hand it to him, and Aaron would light the fire on the altar.

Then one day Nadab and Abihu thought, *We don't have to wait for Dad. We've been helping all this time. Why don't we just go ahead and light the fire on the altar?* So they did.

That's when yesterday's holy fire suddenly became strange new fire and judgment proceeded. The flame from the altar, the blaze they had started, roared forth and consumed them. They both died on the spot.[14] In the end, rebellion will bring death in one form or another to all those who choose to live by it.

SLAVES TO A NEW MASTER

In Scripture we are told to pray, "Our Father in heaven, hallowed be Your name. Your kingdom come,"[15] and soon there are these words: "Deliver us from the evil one."[16]

What we are actually praying is this: "Lord, we acknowledge You are the real King and ultimate authority. But we are constantly attacked by the evil one, who is influencing us to rebel against Your authority. Deliver us from the danger of being deceived into walking away from submission to authority."

Lucifer was given free will to choose, and he chose to disobey. Thus he became Satan, the evil one. Insubordination, rebellion of the heart—this is the method the devil uses to delay and sabotage godliness in the life of a believer.[17] This path of rebellion is a cruel one.

In Genesis we read about Noah, a man whom God sought out from an entire sinful generation. Near the end of his story, we see this godly man get drunk and lie down naked.[18] One of his sons, Ham, saw him in this condition and gossiped about it. Therefore, the descendants of Ham came under a curse. He became a slave.

What was the problem? It was the disrespect Ham demonstrated toward his father, the authority over him. This was no small matter.

Those who show disrespect and refuse to submit to authority ultimately come under a curse and become slaves. They believe they are free, but in truth, they have been brought under bondage. In C.S. Lewis's *The Chronicles of Narnia,* young Edmund resented the authority of his older siblings. Once in the magical land of Narnia, however, there came a time when he thought he had the opportunity to be rid of their authority and become a king. But what looked like freedom turned out to be slavery under an evil master.[19]

Let's look at Absalom.[20] He was a handsome, likeable and brilliant young man. He was the son of King David, a superstar. Then rebellion got a grip on his heart, and he must have thought to himself, *My father, what does he know? He is an old-timer, and I am smarter. He doesn't know how to please the people like I do. I know better.* So Absalom started talking to passersby and giving them his counsel. His actions were filled with pride and false motives. Even so, people believed in him. For quite a while nobody recognized his rebellion; it was private.

Let me ask you a question: With all his brilliance and social skills and so many people looking up to him, was Absalom independent? No. He soon fell under the influence of Ahithophel.

Ahithophel was the closest friend and advisor of King David. Scripture tells us Ahithophel's counsel to David was regarded as God Himself speaking.[21] David would seldom make a decision without the counsel of Ahithophel.

But something sad happened: David committed adultery with Bathsheba, the granddaughter of Ahithophel, and then had her husband killed.[22] God forgave David and cleansed him.[23] But Ahithophel chose not to forgive. His bitterness grew and became as deadly as the venom of a king cobra. He looked for an opportunity to kill David. Then what happened? Ahithophel collaborated with Absalom's rebellion and gave him counsel as to how he could strike David dead. So Absalom became a slave to another's bitterness. In the end, Ahithophel committed suicide, and Absalom was brutally killed.

Please remember that like Absalom, when we privately start spreading rumors, criticizing, attacking and being disloyal to our authorities, we are slowly becoming a slave.

No matter how clever you may be, even if you think you can make it on your own, please keep in mind that no one is free. We all are under authority. If you choose to walk away, you are still not free. The Enemy knows you will need to substitute that authority for another. This is a sobering truth, and hopefully we will all learn from it.

FORFEIT GOD'S BEST?

When we choose the way of rebellion, not only do we end up with a new and evil master, but we also forfeit God's best. The Lord has wonderful plans for all our lives, but when we decide to follow the Enemy's path of insubordination, we miss out on God's best, even in ways we may never know.

Over the past nearly 30 years, I have observed a phenomenon common among those with great potential. Take a young person who is smart and talented. In the beginning, he or she may be given only minor leadership opportunities while waiting for maturity and character to catch up to his or her abilities.

So this person says to himself or herself, *I know what I'm doing! I've read and studied. I can see my way!* This young person sees a leader make a wrong decision and starts to give advice. Because the supervisor graciously receives the suggestion, in the subordinate's eyes his or her importance grows. Self-promotion sets in, and negative comments about superiors begin. Pride and insubordination worsen, and disrespect for leadership surfaces.

Behind the scenes, the leadership team was actually thinking about promoting this person to greater responsibility. After they detected a rebellious attitude, however, they decide this person was not yet ready. Another is promoted, maybe not as smart or capable as the first person, but this individual is humble, broken and loyal. He or she is obedient and submissive.

Unfortunately, often the one with the most brains, instead of using the experience to learn humility, becomes even more arrogant. Until he or she chooses to submit and accept what God has designed, life will continue to unravel while this person thinks all the missed opportunities are someone else's fault. In many cases such an individual may even be asked to leave or will leave on their own, going from one place to another, feeling the world is unjust.

How sad. God was planning a promotion. The leaders intended this. The Lord wanted to use this rising star in a greater degree, but this individual would not submit to God's ways.

Stephen Covey, best-selling author, writes about a "circle of concern" and a "circle of influence."[24] All of us, whether or not we realize it, are focusing on one or the other. The circle of influence is what we can impact and change, and the circle of concern is what we may be troubled about but can't change. If we spend most of our energy focusing on the circle of concern, we most likely end up complaining, murmuring, and even talking against our authorities.

Our circle of influence will then diminish because we are investing our energy on what we can't change instead of what we can. Our opportunity to have a positive influence on what happens around us shrinks instead of grows.

If we focus on altering *our response* to our authorities rather than complaining about their weaknesses, we will not only find ourselves changed, but the attitude of our authority toward us most often changes as well.[25] Likewise, once we submit to what God has for us instead of fighting against it, we will discover His best instead of forfeiting it.

Many years ago there was a man working with me whom I liked a great deal. He was capable and gave up a good job to serve the Lord.

He came to us from another ministry, and I remember asking, "How was your life there?" His response was one of immediate criticism against his former senior leader. I told him, "Please go back and make things right. Maybe what he did was wrong, but please forgive him and let it go. Would you do that? Otherwise it will ruin you."

He responded, "I will."

Some time went by, and we needed to assign a leader for the area in which he was working. I asked my leadership team about putting him in charge. They replied, "You know this brother is quite able, and we know you like him. But his tongue is very sharp. There is also a streak of rebellion in him toward authority." I listened to what they had to say, and we decided instead to put another brother in that key position.

I really wanted to move that man ahead. I believe God also desired to give him a place of greater effectiveness. But in a sense our hands were tied because of the man's choice not to submit to his leaders.

We all want God's best for our lives. But how many times, without even knowing it was right around the corner, have we forfeited what was divinely planned for us? Is doing it our own way really worth it?

NOT BASED ON PERFECTION

We often think that we only need to respect our authorities if they represent our image of what a reputable leader should be like or look like or if they are without glaring faults.

Remember the policeman at the Bombay intersection? He wasn't necessarily a scintillating personality or the most educated individual, but he represented a higher authority. In the same way, those leaders placed over us—parents, husbands, pastors, employers or government leaders—have been appointed by Almighty God to represent His authority. It makes no difference whether they are Nobel Laureates or taxi drivers, good-looking or homely, brainy or simple folk, good-hearted or harsh—they are authorities set there by God for us.

King Cyrus was a Gentile, yet God called him "His anointed."[26] It didn't matter whether or not he was a Jew. He was placed in his position by the living God as His appointed authority.

Those over us will not always do the right thing. That's just a fact of life. As a leader, I know I don't do the right thing all the time. In fact, I make a bundle of mistakes, and I am not proud of it either.

I heard the story of a man who believed he was called to be a prophet. His particular crusade was to expose Christian leaders he thought failed to hold to the right doctrines. He would write articles about them and talk about them. He was not an evil man. He believed he was righteous.

But suddenly he got sick and was paralyzed on one side. During the time of his illness, the Holy Spirit had a chance to speak to him. "If you repent and ask forgiveness from all My servants you have accused and abused, you will be healed," he was told. So this man made phone calls, wrote letters and sought forgiveness from everyone. And God completely restored him.

I am sure all those leaders he accused had their faults. I presume some of the things he said were right on. But they were the Lord's servants, His representatives.

Let's look at the story of Barnabas in the Bible.[27] He is such a nice man. Who doesn't like Barnabas? When no one wanted anything to do with Saul, who came along? It was Barnabas.[28]

With his great reputation for being a giver, a comforter and a wonderful man of God, Barnabas takes Saul, this new believer, under his wing and probably says something like, "Nobody else believes you, but I'm here. I'll be your friend and take care of you." And he actually protects this new Christian.

In the book of Acts, we read about "Barnabas and Saul."[29] Then it changes to "Paul and Barnabas."[30] There was a switch in leadership. Barnabas was more experienced and Paul's senior, but the day came when the Lord picked the radical newcomer Paul to be the leader.

Then an immature disciple called John Mark, the nephew of Barnabas,[31] became part of Paul's missionary team. But on their initial journey, John Mark quit. Maybe he got homesick and wanted to go home.

Before the next trip, however, it appears he came to his Uncle Barnabas and asked if he could go along again. I imagine the conversation went something like this: "Look, I really want to go with you. The Lord called me to serve Him, and I'm sorry about what I did the last time."

"Are you positive you really want to go?" asks Barnabas.

"Yes, I will never leave again! Please, take me with you!"

"I don't know. Let me talk to Paul. He's the boss."

But when Barnabas gets a chance to see Paul alone, he's told, "No way! Absolutely not, and that's final."

"Paul, don't you remember that I'm the one who gave you help? Nobody trusted you!"

"No way. He is not going to be on my team."

We read that there was a strong argument. It might not have been those exact words, but according to the Greek text, it was certainly no casual conversation. The exchange was thunderous. These two men were going at each other. Finally, Paul and Barnabas actually parted ways.

I personally think Paul made a poor choice. He should have been more compassionate toward John Mark. But more important, Barnabas should have submitted to Paul's authority.

Never again do we read about Barnabas. In contrast, God blessed Paul's ministry and used him powerfully to write many of the Epistles we cherish. Don't misunderstand: I am not saying that because Barnabas is no longer mentioned that he was backslidden or became useless in God's work. But the Lord was obviously able to still bless Paul's ministry after the split.

What happened to young John Mark? In 2 Timothy, Paul instructs Timothy to please bring John Mark, "for he is useful to me."[32] Mark is also the one who wrote the Gospel that bears his name. He never could have been the one to do that if he was still bitter against Paul. After the split, he must have taken the disappointment of being rejected and said to himself, *Paul is the leader, and I will not resent his decision.* I imagine Mark submitted with some pain. But he continued to learn and grow, and in time, God obviously lifted him up.

To whom we submit doesn't have that much to do with who is right or wrong, but rather with whom God has appointed as authority.

Consider Noah again. Was it right for Noah to get drunk and lay there naked? No, Noah did wrong. Ham did not lie about his father. Yet his descendants were cursed. Noah's sin revealed Ham's rebellion.

How does this work? Noah's wrongdoing became a test for Ham to see if he would respect the authority over him. Someone once said, "When others do wrong to me, they are in sin. But I am in the will of God." Ham was given the opportunity to do the right thing. His brothers later did the right thing when they took a sheet and walked backward to cover their father. They were blessed.

It is the same way for us. The question is *not* whether those over us do right or wrong but whether we will use the opportunity to revile them—or honor them.

WE MUST OBEY

For 400 years the children of Israel lived in Egypt. Impoverished slaves, mistreated and abused, they cried out to God. In response, the Lord called to Moses and said, "I have certainly seen the oppression of my people in Egypt. I have heard their cries. . . . So I have come down to rescue them" (Exodus 3:7–8, NLT).

God chose Moses as His delegated authority to deliver the 600,000–plus people of Israel from their terrible bondage. Notice that when God said, "I have come down to deliver My people," He meant that He was going to work through Moses.

Freed now from their bondage, they were led by Moses to a "land that flowed with milk and honey."[33] When they came to the border of Canaan, 12 of their senior leaders were sent to spy out the land.

After exploring for 40 days, they returned. Except for Joshua and Caleb, each of the spies gave an evil report about the possibility of possessing this new territory. Their words caused the entire congregation to lose heart.[34]

As a result, "all the Israelites grumbled against Moses."[35] They even talked about *stoning* the delegated authority placed over them! Immediately God entered the scene to deal with their rebellion.

> And all the congregation said to stone them with stones. Now the glory of the LORD appeared in the tabernacle of meeting before all the children of Israel. Then the LORD said to Moses: "How long will these people reject Me? And how long will they not believe Me, with all the signs which I have performed among them? I will strike them with the pestilence and disinherit them, and I will make of you a nation greater and mightier than they" (Numbers 14:10–12).

Then Moses pleaded with God not to destroy them, and He forgave, but God's judgment for rebelling could not be avoided.[36]

> And the LORD spoke to Moses and Aaron, saying, "How long shall I bear with this evil congregation who complain against Me? I have heard the complaints which the children of Israel make against Me. Say to them, 'As I live,' says the LORD, 'just as you have spoken in My hearing, so I will do to you: The carcasses of you who have complained against Me shall fall in this wilderness, all of you who were numbered, according to your entire number, from twenty years old and above'" (Numbers 14:26–29).

Therefore, they all died during the next 40 years while wandering in the wilderness, except for Joshua and Caleb. So the people became slaves to their own words. Before that, the 10 men who instigated the rebellion were struck down by God and died.[37]

God stands behind His delegated authority. He appoints them, and they represent Him. When we disobey, when we make fun of our leaders, we are actually responding directly to God. What a scary thought.

Please don't misunderstand and assume that God is looking for opportunities to judge and hurt people. He's not the author of sin and damnation, sickness, accidents and chaos. God never intended for the children of Israel to suffer and die in the wilderness. He is the One who led them to the land flowing with milk and honey. They were the ones who forfeited His best. It was a choice they made that in the end became the instrument of punishment. But it was not God's plan.

Nevertheless, God doesn't force us to obey. He just waits. If we choose disobedience, He lets us reap the consequences.

The rest of the passage about our delegated authority in Romans 13 reads,

> For rulers are not a terror to good works, but to evil. Do you want to be unafraid of the authority? Do what is good, and you will have praise from the same. For he is God's minister to you for good. But if you do evil, be afraid; for he does not bear the sword in vain; for he is God's minister, an avenger to execute wrath on him who practices evil. Therefore you must be subject, not only because of wrath but also for conscience' sake (Romans 13:3–5).

We are living in difficult times. The independent spirit of Lucifer, the spirit of criticism and arrogance, is at work to undermine leadership. I warn you, God is the same God He was in the Old Testament when He stood with Moses and His servants. I pray that we will learn this and touch godliness instead of the judgment of God. Jesus learned obedience through suffering, and God exalted Him above all names, and He is the Lord of all. May we make that choice as well.

May we learn to live out the Lord's prayer: *Your will be done on earth as it is in heaven. . . . For Yours is the kingdom and the power and the glory forever.*

Dear Lord, we come before You asking for forgiveness. We pray that none of us will be so disappointed with our failures that we don't see Your love. Thank You so much for Your grace. Help us to obey when our authorities hold up that stop sign. Lord, thank You for the opportunity to study Your Word. Use it to transform us so that we live under Your blessing and experience Your best. We trust You, Lord, to do Your work in us. We can't do it without Your help. Amen.

Study Guide for Chapter 5 begins on page 238.

SIX

OUR RESPONSE TO AUTHORITY

We have already covered a good deal of material about submission to authority. Now the question is, What does this look like in our daily lives? Practically, how do we live this out?

There are four major areas of delegated authority that God has established for us: *government, work, church* and *family*. As we examine these specifics, we will have a clear picture of everyday submission.

HIS GOVERNING AUTHORITIES

In the beginning, there was no human government. Adam and Eve alone were given dominion over the earth and all its creatures. God created a perfect world, and prior to the fall, their dominion did not include dealing with the rebellion that Satan would initiate.

But when sin was introduced, everything changed.[1] Self-centeredness, jealousy, hatred and a myriad of other vices became part of the picture. Society could not function any longer without law and order. So God delegated the power of governing fellow men, which is known as the *Dispensation of Human Government*.[2] Then when God called the Israelites out from Egypt, He gave them commandments and ordinances so they would know how to function as a society.[3]

First Peter 2:13–14 says, "Therefore submit yourselves to every ordinance of man for the Lord's sake, whether to the king as supreme, or to governors, as to those who are sent by him for the punishment of evildoers and for the praise of those who do good."

Unfortunately, even among believers, the laws set by our government are sometimes taken lightly. If it seems to us like an inconsequential matter, such as going over the speed limit, it is almost as if obedience becomes optional to us. But God does not view things this way. We are to obey local authorities, even as we should the authority of the nation.

As another example, we should not look for ways to get out of paying taxes. Romans 13:6–7 (NIV) says, "This [their service] is also why you pay taxes, for the authorities are God's servants, who give their full time to governing. Give everyone what you owe him: If you owe taxes, pay taxes; if revenue, then revenue; if respect, then respect; if honor, then honor." We pay taxes because government authorities are in a sense God's workers for society.

God tells us in Exodus 22:28, "You shall not revile God, nor curse a ruler of your people." Not only has God made it clear that we are to obey rulers and the laws they make, but we should not speak against them.

Dr. Billy Graham is a wonderful example of how we should respond to our government leaders. I have watched him more than four decades now. Presidents have come and gone. But as in the case of Daniel, when the kings came and went, he still prospered under each of them.

No matter whether the president was a Democrat or Republican, Dr. Graham always manifested respect for their authority as a great leader in our world. He prayed for them and sought to be a blessing in whatsoever way he could. He could have chosen to criticize some of these authorities when they made mistakes, but he never spoke out against them. He always just made it known that he prayed for them. He is an example for all of us to follow.

HIS AUTHORITY IN THE WORKPLACE

One of the important things to remember when working for our employers is realizing that we are not just serving them, but the Lord. And we don't want to serve Him slothfully, but diligently.

We are under the authority of those we serve. It is our responsibility to obey them and to do as they say, unless they are asking us to sin and dishonor God. Paul says in Ephesians, "Bondservants, be obedient to those who are your masters according to the flesh, with fear and trembling, in sincerity of heart, as to Christ; not with eyeservice, as men-pleasers, but as bondservants of Christ, doing the will of God from the heart" (Ephesians 6:5–6).

God wants us to work as diligently when no one is watching as we would if the boss were there, looking over our shoulder. Not only that, He doesn't want us to work hard just to win favor and have the employer on "our side." Rather, we are to work with a sincere heart out of respect to the Lord, whether or not our employer is pleased with our hard work.

Peter says, "Servants, be submissive to your masters with all fear, not only to the good and gentle, but also to the harsh. For this is commendable, if because of conscience toward God one endures grief, suffering wrongfully" (1 Peter 2:18–19).

It would be easier for us if these verses weren't in the Bible. Whether or not what we do is noticed and appreciated, whether there is kindness or anger from our authority in the workplace, it no longer makes a difference. We do not serve this person for an earthly reward, but for our Lord's sake.

One of the strange things among Christians is the double standard between the secular and religious world. For example, if a person works in the world, they are expected to be on time or they will lose their job. But when in a ministry, sometimes the attitude is that there is "grace" and the sense that they should not be expected to hold to such a standard. I have even heard some say they felt it was more important to come in late but to have spent time with the Lord first. No doubt beginning the day with the Lord is important, yet I can't help but wonder if when serving in the secular world these same individuals wouldn't have found a way to do both. Paul says:

> All who are under the yoke as slaves are to regard
> their own masters as worthy of all honor so that the
> name of God and our doctrine will not be spoken
> against. Those who have believers as their masters

must not be disrespectful to them because they are
brethren, but must serve them all the more, because
those who partake of the benefit are believers and
beloved (1 Timothy 6:1–2, NASB).

Let us please them well in all things, and we will receive a
reward from the Lord.

GOD GAVE US SHEPHERDS

During the 1970s for four-and-a-half years, I pastored a church in
the United States. Then in 1979, as the Lord directed my wife and
me, I resigned from that pastorate to do missions work full-time.

I will always remember that last Sunday. I loved my people, and I
was sad to go. I recall even today the last sermon I preached to my
congregation. It was titled "Seven Things You Must Remember as
I Leave You." One of the points I shared was that whoever was to
follow me as the shepherd of the church—they should obey him
and not hurt him, even if he was a most unqualified person. After
the sermon, many were crying as we said goodbye.

The time came to leave the church that day. Gisela and I, with
our little son Danny, went out of the sanctuary. I distinctly remember walking down the stairs of the church entrance. Down
step one, step two, step three. At the last step, just before I placed
my foot on the road, I suddenly felt like someone was pulling off
my jacket! I turned around. But no one was there. My face went
pale. My wife asked me, "You look strange. What's happened?" I
didn't know how to answer her.

As we were driving away, this revelation came to me: "I placed
you here as the shepherd. Now the mantle I put on you has been

removed. Someone else will take your place."

I was struck with the sacredness of shepherding God's people, and that impression from the Lord has never left me. In fact, in the early days I could not tell this story without choking up.

Now whenever I see a pastor, it doesn't matter how big his church is, his age or what his qualifications are; I recognize I'm dealing with someone who is placed in an important position by the living God to represent Him and shepherd His people. I must honor and respect him and the responsibility God has given him.[4] The New Testament makes it clear that Christ is the head of the Church[5] and that He has appointed shepherds to feed and look after the sheep.[6] Sheep don't lead themselves; the shepherd leads them.

We should have the utmost respect for pastors and the responsibility God has entrusted to them. Paul says to the church in Thessalonica, "Now we ask you, brothers, to respect those who work hard among you, who are over you in the Lord and who admonish you. Hold them in the highest regard in love because of their work" (1 Thessalonians 5:12–13, NIV).

When our pastors speak into our lives, their words should not be taken lightly. If we listen to them and heed their warnings, our lives will be blessed. Obey them and be submissive. Don't fall prey to the attitude of the modern church, which has lost the fear of God and His shepherds.

In the book of Acts, there is a record of a church council meeting. Paul and Peter and others presented their reports and views. Finally James, their spiritual authority, stood up and gave his ruling, and all obeyed and submitted to his decision.[7] "Obey those who rule over you, and be submissive, for they watch out for your souls, as those who must give account. Let them do so with joy and not with grief, for that would be unprofitable for you" (Hebrews 13:17).

HEAVEN IN THE HOME

A home should be a reflection of heaven in its unity, love and peace. Why is heaven such a happy place? Because all beings, even the most powerful archangels, only do what the Father tells them. There is no independent spirit there. All are subject to God's authority.

Just as God designed an order of hierarchy for heaven, He also designed one for marriage and family life. The husband is the head, the wife should submit to her husband and children are to obey their parents.

Just look around—it is not hard to see the confusion and breakup of many homes due to rebellion and lack of submissiveness. If men and women follow God's instructions in the home, however, they will have His blessings and experience a taste of heaven here on earth.

～ Wives, Submit to Your Husbands

In 1 Corinthians 11:3 we read, "But I want you to know that the head of every man is Christ, the head of woman is man, and the head of Christ is God." In our bodies, the head gives direction to the rest of the body. So when the Bible says man is the head of the woman, it means he is the one setting the direction for the family.

From this verse, we know the order of hierarchy is God, Christ, man then woman. God the Father and Jesus Christ are equally divine, yet there is a difference in their roles. One submits to the other. In the same way, man and woman are spiritually equal, but their roles are different. By God's design, one is to lead and the other to follow. So although the wife is not inferior, it is her role to submit to her husband's direction.

Ephesians 5:22 says, "Wives, submit to your own husbands, as to the Lord." Some husbands use this Scripture to force their wives into submission. This is not God's way.

It is the right thing for the wife to submit willingly to her husband. But she does this knowing that she is obeying the living God, for it is God who has asked the wife to submit to her husband.

The principle of headship is something God established from the beginning. It says in 1 Corinthians 11:7, "Woman is the glory of man." Woman was created to manifest man's authority, just as man was made to manifest God's authority. Eve was made for Adam's sake, to be his helper.[8] Obviously the helper follows the one being helped. Before the fall, it was natural for Adam to lead and Eve to follow.

Just as woman's submission is directly linked to creation, it is also tied to the fall. First Timothy 2:14 (NIV) reads, "And Adam was not the one deceived; it was the woman who was deceived and became a sinner." She acted independently, and she was deceived. The fall involved a violation of God-ordained roles for the husband and wife.

Why is the subject of a wife's submission to her husband such a touchy subject? It is due to the curse that came upon mankind through this rebellion and fall. In Genesis 3:16 (NIV) we read the consequence of Eve's sin: "I will greatly increase your pains in childbearing; with pain you will give birth to children. Your desire will be for your husband, and he will rule over you." The word *desire* comes from the Hebrew word *teshuwqah*. In this case, it does not mean "sexual desire," but rather "deep longing for power and control, to be in authority."

The curse is *not* that her husband rules over her, for in the beginning Eve was created to be under Adam's authority. It is her desire to be in control of her husband that is the curse. It should be no surprise, wives, that you find submission to your husbands difficult, for this was passed down to you from Eve, just as pain in childbirth was. This inherited desire, however, does not have to determine the choices you make.

God knows what He is doing, and His ways are always best. As we have discussed earlier, submission is an attitude of the heart. It is *not* simply obedience. It goes beyond that to a desire to understand your authorities and to show them respect and honor.

It is an obvious overstatement, but still it bears saying—men and women are different. Men feel valued and appreciated when they are *respected* and their counsel and advice are taken, whereas women feel valued and appreciated when they sense they are *loved* and are treated with compassion. What if you were to question a man at the workplace, "Do you want people here to respect you or to love you?" He would screw up his face and say, "What do you mean? I am not looking for people here to love me. I want to be respected. I want my dignity."

Nowhere in the Bible does it say, "Women, love your husbands." It says, "Respect your husband. Submit to him."[9] You don't say to a bird, "Fly." It is natural for a bird to fly without having to tell it to do so. The same is true for the wife; it is natural for her to love her husband.

But it is very hard for her to show him respect. A man who knows that his wife loves him may still wonder whether she respects him or trusts his decisions. Look at Ephesians 5:33: "Nevertheless let each one of you in particular so love his own wife as himself, and let the wife see that she *respects* her husband" (emphasis mine).

Dr. Emerson Eggerichs, marriage counselor and speaker, writes, "For so many couples, respect is, indeed, the missing piece of the puzzle."[10] He has received many letters from women writing that everything changed once they took deliberate steps to submit and show respect to their husbands.[11]

Even when a husband is an unbeliever, a wife can win her husband to the Lord through her submission and respect. "You wives, be submissive to your own husbands so that even if any of them are disobedient to the word, they may be won without a word by the behavior of their wives, as they observe your chaste and *respectful* behavior" (1 Peter 3:1–2, NASB, emphasis mine). Obviously, there can be excruciating circumstances in which the situation for the wife is unbearable, and the husband does not respond. Peter did say *may*. More often than not, however, just by being respectful the husband is drawn to the Lord.

What does it look like to respect your husband? Each culture has its own ways of communicating respect. But around the globe, to correct your husband, especially in front of others, is disrespectful to him. Listening to and taking seriously his counsel shows respect. When others are present, not giving your husband any room in the conversation and being the one to answer every question that gets asked is disrespectful. As you seek the Lord, I am confident that He will show you additional ways you can show respect to your husband.

A woman who wants to follow the Lord and please Him will choose to bring her heart under submission to her husband. Scripture says, "[It] is fitting in the Lord" (Colossians 3:18). There is great power behind a wife who chooses to submit to her husband.

—◌ Children, Obey Your Parents

The instruction from the Lord for children is that they obey their parents. In Ephesians 6:1 we read, "Children, obey your parents in the Lord, for this is right." The word used here in the Greek language is *hupakouo*. The way this word is used is not toward an equal, but regarding one who is inferior and needs to obey, for it is the right thing to do.

Children, however, still defy and revile their parents, whether with their words or their hearts, charging, "What do you know? You're old! I know what's right for me." How many sons and daughters are wandering the streets, abused, raped and influenced by evil friends, because they would not submit to their parents?

It is reasonable to think that a 40-year-old has more experience, wisdom and understanding than someone who is 6, 8, 10 or 18. Unfortunately, children are born with a rebellious nature handed down to them from Adam. And parents are meant to be the covering and protection for them.

Now there's something interesting we find in the Gospels. Read these statements from Jesus: "Who is My mother and who are My brothers?"[12] and "Woman, what have I to do with thee?"[13] Jesus lived in subjection to His earthly parents until He left their home for the ministry on which His Father had sent Him. But after He left, He would not do anything until His Father in heaven showed Him that He should go forward.

The same is true in our lives. We must live under submission to our parents as long as we are their dependents. But once we live on our own, it is different. When the Lord has asked you to go forward and your parents disagree, you must obey your Father in heaven, even as Jesus did. But it is wise to take their counsel when it does not oppose what God has clearly asked us to do.

When I wanted to get married, I wrote a long letter to my parents. I remember so well the last paragraph, "Having said all this, Father, I want you to know that I will never go through with this until I hear from you, and you give me your blessing." I still have the letter my father wrote back, granting his permission. Only then did I proceed.

When I was in Germany meeting my future father- and mother-in-law, Mr. and Mrs. Reichart, I told them, "Please know we will not go ahead with our marriage plans until you have given us your blessing." Gisela and I had to wait several months before they chose to do that. As I look back over the years, I have no doubt we have been blessed because we waited for permission and blessing from our parents.

"Children, be obedient to your parents in all things, for this is well-pleasing to the Lord" (Colossians 3:20, NASB). " 'Honor your father and mother,' which is the first commandment with promise: 'that it may be well with you and you may live long on the earth' " (Ephesians 6:2–3).

THE REFLECTIONS OF SUBMISSION

God is not satisfied with just an outward appearance of obedience. He knows that rebellion begins on the inside and is often concealed. There is both passive and active rebellion. Absalom, in the beginning, was passively rebelling. Quietly he was going along, but on the inside, he was already a full-fledged rebel.[14] When someone is passively rebellious, he smiles at you and acts like everything is wonderful, but inwardly he is not submitting.

There the rebellion grows until finally it is exposed.

But God is pleased when our hearts are submitted, and we deliberately choose to place ourselves under the covering He has provided. When we pick that path, it is no longer just external, and we sincerely seek to follow our authorities and respect them. Once we go beyond just copying the proper behavior, positive changes take place that we may not even realize. These are a natural overflow of a heart that is submitted. They are reflections of our yielding to authority.

It is like approaching a mango tree and starting to examine it. "Well, this looks like a mango tree," you say. "All the leaves are correct, but where are the mangoes?" Once you see a mango on the tree, however, you know for sure it's not an apple tree. It is definitely a mango tree. Similarly, when you say, "I submit to authority," there is certain fruit that can be seen in your life—reflections of submission. So, what are some of these reflections of godly submission?

—⁀ Our Body Language

The way we present ourselves before our authority speaks volumes about our attitude toward individuals in positions over us.

There are times when the Lord gives us a picture of one of His principles, and it sticks in our minds as if we took a snapshot of that moment. One of the occasions when the Lord did this for me was when I was a little boy. One morning my mother came to me and said, "Today you are going to kindergarten."

She took me to where my father was sitting in his chair and said, "Touch your father's feet and receive his blessing." I still remember bowing down, touching my father's feet and him putting his hand on my head, saying, "May God bless you, son." That was all he said, but I'll never forget it. It's almost like it took place yesterday. Then we went to the school, and my mother said to me, "Touch your guru's (teacher's) feet and get his blessings." So I did.

Years went by. I finished my schooling and went to North India, then to America and Europe, received my college education and became well established. One day I was back in my little village, Niranam, to visit relatives. As I was walking near the house where I grew up, I came up to an old familiar bridge, and would you believe, here on the bridge comes my first teacher!

He must have been around 80 years old, and he was wearing a *dhoti*[15] and no shirt. I didn't think he would remember me because I looked different. We came face-to-face on the bridge, and I said, "Sir." He responded, "Little one." Then came one of the fondest memories of my life: I bent down and touched the feet of this old man. Here he was standing before me, a skinny, wrinkled old man—my teacher. And I remember him saying the same words to me once again, "May God bless you." I will never forget that encounter.

When we see God's delegated authority as He does, the carelessness in our stance, in the way we sit and in the way we look at the person all begins to change. We realize we are not just responding to anyone, but to the one God appointed over us to represent Him. Our respect carries over into our very posture and conduct.

⌐⌐ Our Words

The Bible instructs us to give honor to those to whom honor is due. When we use titles of respect, like "Sir," "Pastor," "Mr.," "Mrs." and "Dr.," it reflects our respect for authority.[16]

More than the titles we use, our attitude toward authority is communicated through our use of words. Sometimes people refer to their father as "my old man." How sad. When speaking to people who are above you or to elders, always address them with respect. Avoid referring to your superiors as "you guys" or "you people."

Beyond the actual words, our tone of voice, our intonation and the way we ask questions all indicate whether we respect authority. When our hearts are submitted, there's no striving to reach the answer we're looking for. There isn't arguing; instead, there is a deep desire to learn, to understand and to implement completely what is being discussed. All these characteristics are expressed in our words.

─ᴄ Focused Listening

In the same way, you should listen with an attitude of desiring to understand and follow. It's hearing with not only your ears, but also your eyes. They aren't distant eyes that are interested in something else or eyes that are saying, "I already know what you're going to say. You don't have to tell me."

When the prime minister of India, England or Canada or the president of the United States stands before a group of people, do you think anyone is sleeping? No way!

Even beyond hearing what your authority is saying, it is sensing the wishes of this leader, which often means going beyond their actual words and requests. It's being sensitive to them and the situation, not for the sake of your own needs or benefits, but for theirs.

Whether it is our father, mother, husband, pastor, employer, judge or whomever—you should not listen carelessly or flippantly. Listening attentively is a sign of respect.

⟿ Our Appearance

People are careful about how they look when they are involved in some way with a government official! No one with any sense would go before a trial judge in their pajamas. In the same way, your attire should also reflect your respect for all those in authority over you. I cannot enumerate what your situation will always call for. But please be sober about this matter and ask the Lord to show you what this means in your setting.

⟿ Head Covering

Interesting, isn't it? Even at the mention of "head covering," our flesh cringes. It is so interwoven in the spiritual world with submission that it has the same effect on people as the word "submission."

The teaching on "head covering" as a symbol of submission to authority in the life of a woman is mentioned in 1 Corinthians 11:1-16. In the New Covenant life, women are asked to cover their heads in church, especially during prayer time. It is the symbol given to us by God to remember His principle of submission. It is given to women to *do* as a reminder of His government and to men to *see* as His reminder.

We experience God's blessing on our lives when we choose to submit. In the same way, there is a special blessing for the woman who reads this Scripture and chooses to honor the Lord in this way. It is a mystery. It is something we can't explain in human terms. Yet when someone chooses to follow God in this act of obedience, it pleases the Lord.

⌒ A Spirit of Humility

When we seek to honor our authority, we are not wanting to promote ourselves but instead are looking for ways to be a blessing and help. We assume the role of a servant, not acting like we are the one in charge. We look for opportunities to carry their bag or give a glass of water. We give them our chair. Being helpful is always a sign of respect.

No one is perfect, and there may be times the Lord asks us to shed light on a blind spot our authority may have. But when we are submitted, we will do this with a spirit of humility, never with arrogance and a pointing finger. Rather, we'll say, "Look, here is the situation. I may be wrong. Please help me understand if I am mistaken." The intention is not to put down the authority or to make this person look foolish, but rather to help.

⌒ A Transparent Life

When we truly seek to follow our authority, we won't be trying to hide anything. To cover something up implies that we believe we wouldn't have proper approval if our authority knew. If that's the case, then we are not submitting in our hearts. It may not be outright disobedience, but we have certainly not submitted to the overall guidance given. The saying "it is easier to ask for forgiveness than permission" is not God's way.

If we are truly sincere and upright, we will be open and honest with our parents, pastors and leaders. I tell my leaders, "For kindness' sake, I plead with you. Don't hide things from me. Even if you make huge mistakes, I am not angry. But please don't taunt me with half-stories, carefully playing with your words to position yourself in some way. Don't do it."

That kind of behavior demonstrates insubordination, disloyalty and craftiness.

A Desire for Guidance

When we live in submission, we sincerely desire to learn from those God set over us. We watch; we listen; we ask questions. We are even willing to disclose our problems and confide, "Look, this is what I am thinking. I may be completely off the wall. Could you help me or talk to me about it?"

Sometimes we may find ourselves in circumstances in which we don't have an authority figure over us in some realm of our life. It could be because we are in a high level of leadership, or we don't have parents who know the Lord or our father died. In those cases, as one with a submissive heart, we will seek out a mentor, someone who can be an authority over us.

Respectful to Elders

When we have a submitted heart, we respect our elders. These include older brothers and sisters, teachers and our older people. Whether or not they know the Lord, they have journeyed longer than we. Unfortunately, the influence of modern media such as television and movies has fostered disrespect, and the honoring of elders has become a rare gem.

When someone in authority, such as a teacher, walks into a room, everybody stands up and keeps standing until their elder says, "Please be seated." This time-honored custom actually comes from the Bible. "Rise in the presence of the aged, show respect for the elderly and revere your God. I am the LORD" (Leviticus 19:32, NIV). First Peter 5:5 (NIV) says, "Young men, in the same way be submissive to those who are older."

In some cultures, especially throughout Asia, for a younger person or subordinate to sit on the official chair of an elder or leader is seen as disrespectful. When I was growing up, we children were not to sit on our father's chair. My mother would tell us, "That is your father's chair. Don't sit on it."

When visitors or relatives came to our home, no one would sit there. Even when he was not at home, his chair remained vacant. Still today, when I go to any house in any country, I look around to find the chair where the father of the house sits, and I will not sit on that chair. When people insist that I do, I simply explain, "I am sorry. It is out of respect. I cannot do it."

Over the years I have watched young people, with great potential, wreck their lives. One of the main reasons is, even with the call of God and the marvelous gifts He has so graciously given them, they became proud.

Within three to five years, these skilled individuals start thinking they know more than their parents, their pastors and their elders. They no longer seek to learn and understand. The Enemy now has the advantage.

It is like a five-year-old cedar tree. It truly is beautiful. It is the real thing, but it will take another 15, 20, even 30 years before the cedar can be a tree that achieves its unique potential. A young person who understands submission and chooses to respect his or her elders will make it in the end and also be blessed.

─◦ A Heart of Loyalty

When we are truly submitting to authority, one of the evidences will be maintaining loyalty. We won't gossip and pick up the telephone to get our friends to go against our leaders.

Titus 3:1–2 (NIV, emphasis mine) says, "Remind the people to be subject to rulers and authorities, to be obedient, to be ready to do whatever is good, to *slander* no one, to be peaceable and considerate, and to show true humility toward all men."

In my younger days when I was in North India serving the Lord on a ministry team, I was an assistant, and our leader was from Europe. There were seven or eight of us young fellows on the team. More often than not, we had nowhere to sleep except under the trees on the roadside. We sold books to make just enough money to buy some food, and we would preach and then move on to the next area.

But there was a problem. Looking back, I would say that our assigned leader was lacking in leadership skills. Maybe it was that he was from the West and didn't understand what was appropriate in India. Often he got us into these ridiculous situations, though I'm sure now that he didn't realize what he was doing. For me at that time, however, it was absolutely outrageous how he carried out his responsibilities. This made our service hard. I talked to him, but he never really understood.

Then one morning I decided I wasn't going to put up with this any more. So I spoke my mind in front of the whole team. I complained about one thing after another, building my case. For nearly a half-hour, I railed on while the others sat in dead silence. All of a sudden I looked at my leader. He had tears running down his cheeks like small rivers from his eyes. He just sat there.

Suddenly the fear of God came upon me. I realized what I was actually doing. Immediately I stopped and asked, "Would you please forgive me? I have done wrong. Never again will I say one unkind thing about you. This is all wrong."

He didn't change, but I did! That was when I first learned to fear the Lord when speaking against authority. From then on I served this person like a servant. I even covered up the mistakes he made and did my best to protect him. I cannot thank God enough for His mercy in helping me begin to learn this lesson. Later, when I suffered under another leader, I said, "Lord, I am called to submit. I do not know what this will mean in the end. I have no one except You. But I will not open my mouth and attack."

Submitting to our authority is seen in maintaining loyalty even when it results in personal loss and pain.

WRITE THAT LETTER

Just as these reflections indicate a submitted heart, the absence of these characteristics reveals rebellion in our hearts at least to some extent.

If the Lord has convicted you of rebellion against any authority, whomever it might be, I recommend that you make it right. Just settle it. Go and say to that person, "I am so sorry. Would you please forgive me?" That's all you have to do.

Reflect back, and if you have disobeyed your parents, write that email or letter, make that telephone call and be sure you have made things right with them, for it is the way of blessing and it pleases the Lord.

I went back to my authorities and asked forgiveness for the rebellion I carried in my heart. The truth is, I've done this several times. As soon as I realized it was there, I sought forgiveness. I am so glad I did. I know you will be too.

THIS IS THE BEGINNING

As long as the earth remains, there will be seasons—seasons for sowing and seasons for reaping. Often we just want to reap. These are the happiest occasions in life.

As you deliberately choose to submit, the fruit of submission will be in your life. True, there will be some habits in your life that will take time to change. Don't expect instant results. Rather, as you are willing to keep your heart open to God, you will find the seed that has been sown will produce fruit that remains.

Why do I say that? As I look back over almost four decades, I still thank God for that day when I began to learn these principles.

Dear Lord, we are truly humbled when we see all that we have yet to learn. Give us patience as we grow. Lord, we trust You to complete Your work in us. Thank You for Your grace. Amen.

Study Guide for Chapter 6 begins on page 241.

SEVEN

GODLY EXAMPLES OF SUBMISSION

God has given us the Bible to show us how we should live.[1] From beginning to end, it is full of stories of those who have gone before us. These records give us a very tangible look at submission, something that we can actually follow.

It would be like I invited you to my home for dinner. I'd give you directions to my place that explained where to turn and the landmarks you would see. But then something happens. The time comes for you to arrive, but you haven't shown up. My wife has cooked a nice meal, and now the food is starting to get cold.

I'm wondering what's happened, so I pick up my phone and call your cell. "Where are you?" I ask. Glad to hear my voice, you tell me you are lost and can't find the right road. But as you describe your surroundings, I figure out exactly where you are. So I say, "Good. I got it. Wait right there. I'm coming."

I get in my car, and before long, I find you. "Sorry for all the trouble," I say. "Just keep your eyes on my 1962 yellow Volkswagen Bug and follow me back to my house."

So now you don't have to look at the map or the street signs. You just need to concentrate on the back of my little car. I lead and you follow, and within 10 minutes of making all the right turns, this way and that, we drive up to my house.

"Oh, that was easy," you say.

Why was it easy? Because all you had to do was follow.

The Apostle Paul told the Corinthians, "Follow my example, as I follow the example of Christ" (1 Corinthians 11:1, NIV). If you want to learn the ways of God, if you want to touch godliness, if you want to avoid sin and disaster, go to the Bible and read about the people God has given to us as examples. Follow their successes and avoid their failures.

There are many individuals in Scripture who truly demonstrated what it means to submit to authority in spite of suffering and loss. Let's study the lives of just a few of these people.

MIGHTY MAN OF GOD

Paul, the Apostle[2]—from a distance, he may come across as a self-made man who doesn't bend before anyone or anything. But that's really far from the truth. Paul was a broken, humble man who learned to live a life of submission before both God and man. And this was the key to God committing Himself to Paul.

Before he was the Apostle, he was Saul of Tarsus—a Pharisee, and as for legalistic righteousness, he was faultless.[3] He was of the highest caste in society with both financial backing and a great education. Self-righteous, he was convinced that he was doing the right thing by killing Christians and opposing this Christ everyone was talking about.

But then on the road to Damascus, he met Jesus Christ Himself. There he was struck down with a bright light, and he heard those words, "Saul, Saul, why are you persecuting Me? . . . It is hard for you to kick against the goads."[4]

Saul immediately asked, "Who are You, Lord?"[5] By calling Him *Lord,* Saul was saying in the literal sense of the word that he now belonged to the One he was addressing.

"I am Jesus,"[6] was the response he heard.

Saul was dumbfounded. "Lord, what do You want me to do?"[7] he stammered. His question was the beginning of a life of absolute surrender.

God instructed Saul to go to the city of Damascus. There, He said, "you will be told what you must do."[8] Think about this for a second. All Saul knows to do is to go to Damascus. God didn't tell him where to go in the city or how long he would have to wait or even how he was to know the next step.

Then when Saul gets up, he opens his eyes and can't see a thing. He is absolutely blind. Now the mighty, intelligent, rich and famous "Saul of Tarsus" has to be led by the hand like a child. In order for him to submit to his new Lord, he has to humble himself and take this road of brokenness. For three days, he waits sightless and helpless. God was using these first steps in submission to train Saul in godliness.

Next the Lord made contact with Ananias, a disciple living in Damascus. He gave him Saul's address and told him to make a house call. The Lord adds, "He is a chosen vessel of Mine to bear My name before Gentiles, kings, and the children of Israel. For I will show him how many things he must suffer for My name's sake" (Acts 9:15–16).

The Lord could have done everything for Saul Himself. He could have opened his eyes, baptized him and filled him with the Holy Spirit. Instead, God chose to work through His delegated authority. It was Ananias who was divinely appointed to bring Saul healing and to guide him at this point in his journey. God was saying to Saul, "Submit yourself under My delegated authority." Saul, who was such an intelligent, capable individual, had to put his life in the hands of Ananias, a simple unknown man mentioned only once in the Bible. Even so, Saul submitted to what was required of him, because he had met his ultimate Authority on the road to Damascus.

God stood by Ananias. When he laid his hands on Saul, the scales immediately fell off his eyes. Once blind and helpless, Saul now received back his eyesight. As he submitted to this simple disciple of Christ, he got what he so desperately needed—sight and insight.

As the days progressed, Saul increased in both strength and influence. It was obvious that God's hand was upon his life and that His blessing was upon Saul's ministry.[9]

From Damascus he traveled to Jerusalem so he could spend time with Peter. He followed the former fisherman for two weeks, going wherever he went.[10] He took the time to seek out and learn from those who were his elders in the proclamation of Christ.

Saul was an intelligent and gifted leader. He was a man of influence and importance even before he knew Christ. When he submitted to Jesus and His delegated authority, he by no means laid down his great skills and simply became a doormat, as some view submission. He was a pioneer and brilliant leader. He did not lose his abilities and charisma in this process; he simply let God now channel these resources His way instead of Saul's own way.

As this new champion of the faith spoke boldly among the Jews in Jerusalem, some sought to kill him, so the apostles sent him back to Tarsus. There he remained for a number of years until Barnabas came to get him to minister as a team in Antioch.

After a year of church work, the Holy Spirit said to the local leaders during a prayer meeting to separate Saul for the work to which God had called him. They could have exclaimed, "What are You talking about, God? You already called him. He is already separated."

Once again God chose to work through His authority in that setting. Even with a mighty individual like Saul, God still essentially said, "I cannot work except through the authority I have established." So the church leaders laid hands on him and sent him out.

Now known as Paul the Apostle, he was preaching the Gospel not only in synagogues, but also among the Gentiles, planting churches everywhere he went. There came a time when he and his co-workers needed to know how God wanted them to handle the new Gentile converts. It was decided that Paul and Barnabas and a few other leaders should go to Jerusalem to the apostles and elders and seek their guidance.

All through the New Testament, we see Paul talking to God and having direct access to Him. Why didn't the Lord just tell him what to do? After all, many of these people came to Christ under Paul's teaching. Why didn't the apostle just figure this out on his own? Instead, Paul and some of his colleagues take the time to travel back to Jerusalem and present the problem to the church leaders in authority.

James the brother of Jesus and the apostles and elders listen to what has happened regarding the many Gentile believers. Then James, the senior leader, speaks up and gives a ruling.

After James announces his decision, Paul never opens his mouth. He took this ruling as from God and went on establishing His work.

Paul faced opposition every place he went. This resistance came primarily from the Jewish religious community, but as we read through Acts, we see that quite often it was the government that provided his protection.[11] For example, when he was in Corinth, the Jews accused him before the governor Gallio. Before Paul even had a chance to speak, Gallio told the Jews, "I don't have time to listen to your own laws."[12] And he made them leave the court.

The same basic scenario is repeated throughout Acts. The Lord even used Paul's imprisonment in Jerusalem as a protection from imminent death threats and as a means for him to speak to the courts and monarchs of the day. Whether these leaders in government realized it or not, their decisions were directed by God to accomplish His purposes. From the beginning when God spoke to Ananias, He foretold that Paul was to speak before kings. If Paul had rebelled against these governmental leaders, he would have forfeited a part of God's plan for him.

When Paul was later on trial in Jerusalem, the high priest

Godly Examples of Submission

Ananias told someone near Paul to strike him on the mouth. Paul immediately reacted with truthful criticism. Those who stood by said, "Do you revile God's high priest?"[13]

Paul quickly replied, "I did not know, brethren, that he was the high priest; for it is written, 'You shall not speak evil of a ruler of your people.' "[14] The high priest must not have been wearing his official dress, and Paul did not recognize who he was. Obviously Paul was *more* concerned about his lack of respect toward the high priest than he was about being slapped in the face and humiliated in front of everyone.

Submission often includes difficulties, pain and suffering in the flesh, but it brings a life of peace and freedom. When Paul was waiting for two years for a verdict from Felix, he knew the Lord's purpose was for him to go to Rome. As he submitted to the Lord and to His authorities, he could be at peace knowing that the Lord would bring it to pass.

After years of submitting himself to God and his authorities, Paul was able to say at the end of his life, "I have fought the good fight, I have finished the race, I have kept the faith" (2 Timothy 4:7).

A MAN AFTER GOD'S OWN HEART

One of the most significant examples we have of submission to authority is found in the life of King David.[15] He actively pursued submitting to his delegated authority even in the midst of devastating personal crisis. This choice was a beautiful reflection of his heart of submission toward His Lord.

David's story begins with Saul, Israel's first king. Saul started out as a good ruler and battled strong for Israel. Early on he called for war on the Philistines. But the opposition had a better turnout than Saul expected, and his men began deserting.

King Saul got impatient waiting for Samuel the priest to show up to perform the required sacrifice. So he did what he should have never done and performed the sacrifice himself. Just as he finished, Samuel arrived on the scene.

He reported to Saul, "The LORD has sought out a man after his own heart and appointed him leader of his people, because you have not kept the LORD's command" (1 Samuel 13:14, NIV). That leader in the wings was David. The Lord knew this young man's heart and picked him out from all those in Israel.

Samuel was grieved that Saul had dishonored the Lord, and the man of God kept stewing about it. But the Lord told him, "Forget about Saul. I have chosen someone else. Go and anoint David to be king."[16] So Samuel went to Bethlehem and poured his sacred oil on the youngest of Jesse's eight sons. From that day forward, the power of the Lord's Spirit was upon this young man.

At the same time, the Spirit of the Lord departed from Saul, and he was demonized. The king's attendants realized what happened to Saul and suggested that someone come and soothe his spirit by playing the harp. In what was more than a coincidence, David was recommended. And Saul approved this action! So now, here was David in direct service to his king, and Saul really liked him. This new man also became one of the king's armorbearers. David not only faithfully played the harp for Saul, but he also sought to serve him in any way he could.

Goliath the Philistine began boasting before the Israelites, and David boasted of the Lord and killed this giant with a stone. The rest of the Philistines ran from the Israelites. That day of victory there was happiness and elation, singing and dancing all throughout Israel. Though praise went to Saul, even more was directed David's way. Saul heard about David's popularity. But instead of raising his hands and honoring God for such a helper, Saul became terribly upset. He was filled with jealousy to the point that he decided to kill David.

The next day, as David was playing the harp for his king as he normally did, instead of being comforted, Saul became angry. He flung his spear across the room at David—not just once, but twice. Each time David dodged the attack.

If I were David, I probably would have quit right then and there. Instead, he remains in Saul's service. Yes, God had rejected Saul and already anointed David as the nation's next king, but Saul was still the one on the throne. How could David just walk in? He couldn't. Even in this difficult situation, for David to oppose Saul would be to reject God Himself.

The more David submitted, the more pliable he became in the Lord's hands. His choices of submission were not easy by any means. They required suffering and faithfully serving someone who was no longer thinking normally. But David stayed the course.

Saul then decided, "I won't kill him. I'll let the Philistines do it."[17] But there David's life was preserved by God. Again David submitted to Saul as he would to God. He did everything with all of his heart, and the Lord gave him great success. The Philistines continued to go after the Israelites, but David met them with a string of victories. The result was that all of Israel and Judah loved him all the more.

Saul realized that if David's successes continued, this young fellow would soon have his job. He was afraid of this and became even more determined to kill David. Once again, the king's helper had to duck Saul's flying spear. And this time, David removed himself from Saul, but not in rebellion.

He first went to Samuel. David told him everything that was going on. I have no doubt that he also sought his wisdom and counsel. Who knows, maybe it was during this time with Samuel that David gained the wisdom and strength to respond to Saul as he did in the following days.

When Saul heard where he was, David fled. He was still on the run when his brothers joined him. Even in the midst of fleeing for his life, David considered his parents. Now that his brothers were with him, there was no one to watch over them. So he went to the King of Moab and asked if he would let his father and mother live with him until things got worked out.

While in Moab the prophet Gad told him, "Do not stay in the stronghold. Go into the land of Judah."[18] He respected this prophet and left Moab.

Saul chased David all over the place trying to kill him. He had 3,000 well-trained and strong soldiers. It was like assigning 3,000 troops to kill a stray dog! Yet day after day, the Lord protected David from his master.

Imagine running for your very life for a whole day. It's a scary thought. Now think about having to do this for years. And consider that it's not from some troublemaker in society, but from your own leader, whom you have served with all your heart. Even when David had every reason to be rebellious against and disrespectful of Saul, he chose not to do so, but rather to forgive and to show respect.

One day during this chase, David and his men were hiding out in the back of a large cave. Would you believe Saul happens into that same cave to go to the bathroom? David's men whisper, "Look, David, God said He would deliver your enemy into your hand to do to him as you wish. Now's your chance. Kill him."[19]

David quietly sneaked up to Saul and cut off a corner of his robe. Why didn't he take his tormentor's life? He had God's word to support his case. All the circumstances lined up. Everything looked correct. The only thing for David to do—by logic and his feelings of self-preservation, the thought of fulfilling God's will for His people, and following the unanimous advice of his men—was to go ahead and strike Saul dead. But David knew something deeper, more holy. He looked at the situation from God's perspective of submission to authority.

He must have said to himself, *Though this man is backslidden and demonized, Saul is still God's anointed. I must not raise my hand against him.* So David chose to go against his human reasoning and honored his authority. What a mystery of godliness.

David went back to his men and told them there was no way he would do anything against the king and that no one was to harm him. He even felt guilty for cutting Saul's royal robe. Even in private, you never hear David speaking against Saul or allowing others to criticize him. He backs him up even after all he has gone through.

Saul walks out of the cave and back to his grisly business. Then David calls after him, "My lord the king!"[20] When Saul turned to look back, there was David with his face to the ground, bowing to him, humbling himself before his king.

What an amazing example of a man who understood the godliness of not reviling authority. Instead of making this an opportunity to criticize, David took it as another time to honor him. Here are his amazing words to Saul (my paraphrase):

> "Don't listen to anyone who is telling you that I want to harm you. Today I was in the cave with you and others urged me to take this as an opportunity from God to kill you. But I cannot stretch out my hand against my lord, the Lord's anointed. Look, my father, I have part of your robe in my hand. I cut it off, but I did not hurt you. Please see that there is no evil or rebellion in my heart toward you. I have not sinned against you, yet you want to kill me. Let the Lord judge. But my hand will not be against you. I am confused about this whole thing. You are the king of Israel, yet you are pursuing me. . . . But what am I but a dead dog? A flea?"[21]

Saul responded, "Is that your voice, David my son?"[22] Then Saul started weeping openly and said, "You have treated me well, but I have treated you badly. . . . When a man finds his enemy, does he let him get away unharmed?"[23] Then Saul returned home, but David and his men stole away to a safe place. David respected Saul and did not take advantage of this opportune moment, and Saul, at least temporarily, changed his attitude and returned home.

As time passes, Saul again takes up the pursuit of David. Instead of cutting off a piece of his robe, this time David takes his spear and water jug. The Lord puts Saul and his army into a deep sleep, while David creeps in quietly under the cover of night.

As David and his friend stand over the sleeping Saul, David says, "I am not going to harm him. The LORD can kill him or a day will come that he will die whether by old age or battle. But I am not going to do it" (1 Samuel 26:10–11, paraphrased).

David trusted God implicitly for his future.[24] He believed that if he honored his authority, in the end the Lord would somehow accomplish His purpose. He was being prepared to be in a place of authority by truly honoring those God had placed over him.

In time the Israelites faced another struggle with the Philistines. The battle was fierce, and Saul's three sons were killed. The king was severely wounded and actively pursued. At this point he chose to take his own life.

A man from Saul's camp searched for David. He told him that the Israelites had lost the battle and that Saul and Jonathan were both dead. David asked him how he knew this was so. The messenger explained that Saul was leaning on his spear, half dead, and had called him over to finish the job. "So I stood over him and killed him, because I was sure that he could not live after he had fallen. And I took the crown that was on his head and the bracelet that was on his arm, and have brought them here to my lord" (2 Samuel 1:10).

When David heard the news of Saul's death, he was not happy or relieved. Rather, he broke down weeping for Saul and Jonathan. In this scene of mourning, something strange happened. David asked the young man who gave him the news, "Where are you from?"[25]

He answered, "I am the son of an alien, an Amalekite."[26]

Then David asked him, "Why were you not afraid to lift your hand to destroy the Lord's anointed?" (2 Samuel 1:14, NIV).

Then David called one of his young men and commanded, "Go . . . execute him!"[27]

Later David learned that the men of Jabesh Gilead had retrieved Saul's body and buried it. He sent messengers to say, "The LORD bless you for showing this kindness to Saul your master by burying him. May the LORD now show you kindness and faithfulness, and I too will show you the same favor because you have done this" (2 Samuel 2:5–6, NIV).

Even in Saul's death, David had great respect for this authority God placed over him.

David never tried to bring to pass what God had promised him. "In the course of time, David inquired of the LORD. 'Shall I go up to one of the towns of Judah?' he asked. . . . 'Go up. . . . To Hebron,' the LORD answered."[28]

So David went to Hebron with all his men and their families, and they settled there. Then the men of Judah gathered in Hebron and anointed him king over the house of Judah.

Seven years later, all Israel came together to David at Hebron and said, "We are your own flesh and blood. In the past, while Saul was king over us, you were the one who led Israel on their military campaigns. And the LORD said to you, 'You will shepherd my people Israel, and you will become their ruler' " (2 Samuel 5:1–2, NIV).

It was then that all the elders of Israel anointed David king as the Lord had promised years earlier through Samuel. David was 30 years old when this happened,[29] and he became more and more powerful because the Lord Almighty was with him.[30]

David was faithful to honor and respect his authority through all those years of rejection, misunderstandings, betrayal and loneliness, with the king and his soldiers running after him. Still the Lord brought him through all this suffering to a place of godliness and blessing. His fame spread through every land, and God made all the nations fear him.[31]

Nathan the prophet came to David to give him a wonderful word from the Lord: "I took you from the pasture and from following the flock to be ruler over my people Israel. I have been with you wherever you have gone, and I have cut off all your enemies from before you. Now I will make your name great, like the names of the greatest men on the earth. . . . Your house and your kingdom will endure forever before me; your throne will be established forever" (2 Samuel 7:8–9, 16, NIV).

Submission is the way God accomplishes His eternal purposes. In the measure that David submitted, in that same measure he experienced God's restoration and life of blessing. In Acts 13:22, the Lord says of David, "I have found David the son of Jesse, a man after My own heart, who will do all My will." David obeyed God and his delegated authorities through incredible turmoil. It is no wonder his throne is established forever. Down through the ages, even as God promised, David is still known as one of the greatest men who ever lived on this earth, and his kingdom endures forever.

GOD'S FAITHFUL SERVANT

Joseph was another man of many trials, but as he submitted in each situation, he learned obedience. And this strange path eventually led him to the position of prime minister of Egypt.

Joseph's story[32] begins with his father, Jacob. He loved Joseph more than the rest of his sons. Joseph's 10 older brothers were aware of this, and they hated Joseph for it. They gave him a hard time whenever they could and had almost nothing kind to say to him or about him. Yet he learned to submit to their ill treatment.

Initially Joseph was not all that wise in his dealings with his brothers. Early on, he had dreams about them someday bowing down before him. Instead of keeping this to himself, he told his father and his siblings, which made his brothers dislike him even more. His father chided him, "Don't you have any sense in your head? What are you talking about? Your brothers and your parents, we are all going to bow down before you?"[33]

Yet Joseph had an obedient spirit. One day his father said, "Your brothers are off feeding the flocks. Why don't you go and find out how they're doing?"[34]

Joseph replied, "Here I am,"[35] and off he went. He obeyed his father without question. If I were Joseph, having experienced the kind of mean-spiritedness he had received from his brothers, I would have been careful not to put myself in such a dangerous position. But his father said it, so he just obeyed and went.

Spying him coming from a long way off, his brothers devised an evil plan. "Here comes that dreamer!"[36] they mocked. "Let's kill him and . . . then we'll see what comes of his dreams."[37]

When Joseph arrived, they grabbed him, tore off his coat and threw him into a nearby pit. The Lord protected him, however. Instead of being murdered, he was sold as a slave. Yet Joseph didn't fight or curse them. Filled with emotion, he pleaded and begged, "Have mercy, please. Let me stay!"[38]

Can you imagine this young "favorite of his father" now being marched off to the strange land of Egypt with its different language and strange culture? I have no doubt that Joseph shed bitter tears on his journey. Though he knew his brothers didn't like him, I don't believe he ever expected they would actually do something like this. After all, they were his older brothers, his very blood.

Yet he submits to what happens. I suppose Joseph may have said, "God, I don't know what to do. I obeyed my father, my authority, and now I'm caught in this dreadful situation." The most loved son now became a slave to Potiphar. God was using these events to train Joseph in godliness. He learned to submit at home in the midst of bitterness and hate, and he would now have to learn submission as a slave.

We don't read anywhere that Joseph told Potiphar and his wife, "This is the whole story of how I got sold into slavery." If he was bitter and unforgiving toward his last delegated authority (his older brothers), most likely he would have eventually carried that over toward Potiphar. But from the biblical account, we have every reason to believe that Joseph served Potiphar out of a sincere heart.

Though everything had gone against him, instead of complaining, Joseph forgave and now served his new authority with all of his heart. This attitude not only gave him hope, but his new authority Potiphar was pleased with him.

The Lord was certainly with Joseph too. The young man worked hard, served diligently and started to become quite successful. Potiphar saw it, and soon Joseph became the head man of the house. Everything was put under his authority. Potiphar trusted Joseph so much that he didn't even have to check on what Joseph did. He just left everything for Joseph to take care of, to the extent that Potiphar hardly even knew what he had, except for the food he ate each day.

But again the vibrant, healthy, mature, handsome Joseph ends up in trouble. Usually it's the man who lusts after the woman, but not in Joseph's case. Potiphar's wife goes after him. Joseph tells her, "Look, my master ... has committed all that he has to my hand ... [except for] you. .... How then can I do this great wickedness?" (Genesis 39:8–9). Obviously to yield to the temptation was wrong, but even beyond the moral sense, Joseph knew that doing such a thing would violate his master's trust.

Day after day he was enticed by this attractive lady of the house, until finally he literally ran from her. Instead of Joseph being rewarded for his commitment, Potiphar accused him of the very thing from which he had fled.

Potiphar, who was a powerful official, had Joseph thrown into prison. For his choice of submission, Joseph suffered misunderstandings, inconveniences, pain and humiliation.

Through all this, however, we never read a word of accusation against his brothers or Potiphar and his wife. All we ever hear Joseph say is, "I was stolen away from the land of the Hebrews; and also I have done nothing here that they should put me into the dungeon" (Genesis 40:15). Apparently, he didn't spell out vivid descriptions of his heartache and pain.

In the midst of the injustice, suffering and waiting, God was still with him. I'm sure the Lord suffered with him and, in that sense, was saying, "I understand, Joseph." Joseph's response to God could have been, "If you understand, why are You allowing me to go through all this pain and agony?" But Joseph trusted God and waited to see what He had planned.

Even while Joseph was in prison, the Lord was able to convey His mercy and favor toward him. The warden soon committed all the prisoners into Joseph's care, and everything in the jail was by his doing. Once again he prospered, and he was learning to submit not only as a slave, but also as a prisoner. Joseph needed this time to grow into filling the high position he would eventually hold.

Thirteen long years go by[39]—years of faithfully submitting in a hot Egyptian prison—but in the end Joseph is brought to the place of blessing. God places a dream in the mind of the sleeping Pharaoh. Who is asked to interpret it? You guessed it! So Joseph tells the ruler what's to come and how to prepare for it in the years of plenty. The Pharaoh himself realizes he needs someone who will watch over his land during this process and exclaims, "Can we find such a one as this, a man in whom is the Spirit of God? . . . You shall be over my house, and all my people shall be ruled according to your word; only in regard to the throne will I be greater than you. . . . See, I have set you over all the land of Egypt" (Genesis 41:38, 40–41).

Joseph is promoted to prime minister of the most powerful nation at the time. Now he faithfully serves Pharaoh. And the ruler trusts his prime minister and tells his people, "Go to Joseph, and do whatever he tells you."[40] Even though Joseph had authorities in the past who wronged him, he continued to serve faithfully those God put over him.

More years go by. Joseph's brothers, faced with worldwide famine, journey to Egypt to buy food. They come before Joseph and bow down before him, but with no clue as who he really is. Joseph looked different now. He was older and more mature, and he wore Egyptian clothing. On top of that, he was in authority.

As Joseph recognized his brothers, his emotions welled up. He couldn't handle them, and he ran back to a room and wept. What was he weeping about? Was it past bitterness, anger and frustration? Was it because of their cruelty and the lost years? No. He was weeping out of love and emotion. "My brothers, my blood. Oh, they are here!" He was eager for information. He asked all kinds of pointed questions and wanted to know how his father was. "What's happening? Tell me!"[41]

In the end Joseph told his brothers, "Please don't think I am going to do anything wrong to you. You sold me into slavery, but God sent me here ahead of you, knowing that this time of famine would come and that I would need to be here to help my family—to help you. So it really wasn't you who sent me here; it was God. See what He has done" (Genesis 45:5–8, paraphrased).

Joseph gives them provision to go back to their homeland and bring their father and all his household down to Egypt. Then he provides for his father and for all of his brothers during this time of famine.

Once Jacob dies, Joseph's brothers are afraid he might now pay them back. But he tells them, "Am I in the place of God? . . . You meant evil against me; but God meant it for good. . . . Do not be afraid; I will provide for you and your little ones" (Genesis 50:19–21). Joseph's submission to God and his delegated authority brought him rest from worry and bitterness. Even though Joseph's authorities, his older brothers, had once wronged him, in his mind it was God who ultimately orchestrated what happened, and through it He had spared the promised people of Israel, accomplishing His purpose.

Before Jacob died, he had said of Joseph, "The archers have bitterly grieved him, shot at him and hated him. But his bow remained in strength, and the arms of his hands were made strong by the hands of the mighty God of Jacob" (Genesis 49:23–24). As Joseph submitted instead of reacting or fighting, God continually strengthened him and provided what ultimately was best both for him and his whole family.

THREE-DIMENSIONAL SUBMISSION

What outstanding pictures these are of submission to authority. Here were men who feared God and practiced submission even when it seemed everything went against them. It was not because they were inferior or unable to make their own plans. They chose to submit because they knew that ultimately they were bending their knees before the throne of God. They did all that they did for Him.

They all worked hard so their authorities never had to watch over them, because their real master was God. Even when their authorities made wrong choices or were outright sinful, they submitted as best they could. They laid aside their agendas, their fears and their own well-being and chose to submit.

In similar fashion, as long as we try to save our own lives, we will lose them. But if we give them away, let them be, submit and surrender, then we will truly find them. [42] Those who testify to a genuine deeper encounter with God all experience this brokenness and humility that result from submission.

You see, submission always starts with the choice that it is no longer what we wish or what we want. We only desire His will. This means we have chosen to walk the road of brokenness— the catalyst that breaks up the fallow ground of our souls. It is by bending our necks that we submit to the yoke of authority. When we do this, our eyes of understanding are opened to see clearly the ways of God.

God dwells in two places. One is heaven, and the other is the heart of someone who has a broken and contrite spirit.[43] The Bible reports that in these three men's lives, God was with them and that they increased and were successful.[44] It is not by chance that God chooses to align Himself with someone. It is with the humble, with the broken, that God resides in power.

Through submission they truly experienced God's blessing, but it was not without intense suffering. The two go hand in hand. God used all of the events in their lives to mature them for greater usefulness and the fulfillment of His plans for them.

Joseph was willing to submit even when he ended up in prison for years. He suffered without murmuring against God. He didn't say a mean word against the older brothers who mistreated him. He never spoke against Potiphar and his wife. And God used those experiences to train him. Although Joseph suffered in prison for 13 years, he was the prime minister of Egypt for 43 years.

Look at David—anointed king as a young man yet years go by and he's still not on the throne. If he had then been asked, "David, where is your throne? Where is your crown?" he likely would have replied, "I am under training."

God always has our best in mind, to bless us and make us a blessing. And His anointing on the lives of these men was a direct result of their submission. It was through this that God was able to accomplish His eternal purposes.

This principle of submission to authority is not an earthly one. It is an eternal principle, sacred and holy. To the extent anyone embraces it, they will see God come to their side. He will make sure they will be not the tail, but the head.

As it reports in 1 Corinthians 10:11, the stories of these lives were written down for our example. May God help us follow their example.

*D*ear Lord, please help us hear from You. Thank You for the testimonies of Paul and David and Joseph, that we may follow in their footsteps. Help us to walk in humility and sincerity before You and the authorities You have given us. Our desire is to please You. Thank You for Your mercy toward us when we are slow to learn. Don't allow us to give up on this journey toward submission. We trust You, Lord, that You will complete us. We pray this in the name of Jesus, the greatest of all examples. Amen.

Study Guide for Chapter 7 begins on page 244.

EIGHT

WHY WE REBEL

We have journeyed far. We have looked upon the earth's first days when Adam and Eve chose to disobey and thus submitted their lives to the influence of Satan.[1] We went back further still and watched as Lucifer, through his insubordination, became Satan.[2] Even before time began, we eavesdropped on the secret councils of the Trinity when the Son chose to be second and to submit to God the Father.[3]

We saw how Jesus came to earth to suffer as He learned obedience and displayed God's intention for man in humility and submission. We also looked at the lives of godly individuals who though for a time endured great hardship in their obedience, reaped divine protection over their lives and blessings beyond anything we would expect.

Then we have been confronted with the reality that when we rebel against our delegated authorities, we are actually rebelling against God Himself. Judgment follows. When we submit to our delegated authorities, however, we submit to God Himself and please Him. And by this choice, we show how much we love Him.

It is obvious that this principle of submission to authority is not only significant but sacred to God. So much of what happens in our lives hinges upon this one important principle.

So now here's the question: If this truth is so significant, why don't we want to submit? Why is there so much rebellion? Even the word *submission*—who likes it? Especially in this generation, from day one children are encouraged to be strong and independent.

Why are we so blind? The god of this world influences mankind through his power. Paul calls Satan "the ruler of the kingdom of the air, the spirit who is now at work in those who are disobedient" (Ephesians 2:2, NIV). It is always our own choice, but more often than not, Satan is whispering in our ear, convincing us to give in to the ways of rebellion.

What are the "reasons" why we yield to his influences?

IT STARTS IN OUR MIND

Our mind is the battleground. Watchman Nee writes, "Rebellious words come from rebellious reasoning, and reasoning in turn is 'cooked up' in thought. Hence thought is the central factor in rebellion."[4] It all begins with our thoughts and imaginations, which too often are influenced by Satan. These thoughts then become "fortresses" that end up blocking our understanding of God's ways in the situation at hand.

This is where our ancestors lost that first battle to the devil. When he talked with Eve, Satan appealed to her mind and emotions, saying, "You will be like God. He knows what's going to happen if you eat of this fruit. You will know what is right and wrong. That will make Him jealous."⁵ So Eve started thinking about this.

You can just imagine what went on in her mind: *Is that true? I didn't realize that. I mean, what could be so bad about eating this fruit?* Reasoning with her mind, she decides to take a bite instead of saying, "Okay, God, I believe You. You said not to do this, so that settles it. I will obey." Instead, she tried to figure things out *in herself.*

What Eve was not able to understand was that God wasn't worried about the apple or the mango. He created a multitude of trees and plants. What was so important about this one little fruit? The crux of the matter was that God placed Adam and Eve under His authority so they would learn obedience. He didn't make them do it. He gave them the freedom to choose. But Eve's thought to become like God became a fortress that blocked her understanding of Him. She wasn't able to see beyond her reason and logic to His greater plan for her.

Just as a wife might think to herself, *This husband of mine is not smart. He can't make wise decisions, so I am going to take charge now. I will start making the decisions.* Good logic, but God looks upon it and says, "You don't understand. It is not about how smart or dumb he is. It is about you being under his authority."

Before Adam and Eve fell, right and wrong were in God's hand. Whatever God said, that was all they knew. When they ate the fruit of the tree of knowledge of good and evil, they found the source of right and wrong in something other than God Himself. *Innocence died.*

We are all the children of Adam and Eve. No longer innocent, we are born independent from God. Untold numbers of Christian workers are living in rebellion to their authority because they "reason" within themselves to see if what their leader is doing is good or bad as far as they understand it. Watchman Nee said, "Man's action should not be governed by the knowledge of good or evil; it should be motivated by a sense of obedience."[6]

How many times have you said to yourself, *What you say is right, but I know better*? I had a professor in college, Dr. Macbeth. One time he made this funny statement: "I wish children were parents first before they became children." Children think that they are smarter and more intelligent than their parents and that they know what is best. Then they grow up, get married and have sons and daughters—who think the very same thing! These parents say the same thing their own parents did: "You think you're smarter? Don't you realize I've lived longer than you have?" But the children don't value their parents' counsel because they believe they are capable of knowing right and wrong for their own lives.

We all think we know what is best for us. We assume we are able to distinguish good from evil. But we are deceived. Eve was also deceived by Satan. In a similar way, when we try to argue and reason, we too can come under the deception of demons.

If you study people who are in rebellion, you find the underlying reason for their attitude is that their way makes sense in their natural mind. I have been serving the Lord for almost 40 years, and I have dealt with many blatantly rebellious people. Of the hundreds I have known, seldom was I able to help someone come to a place of repentance, saying, "I never saw that. Will you please forgive me? Will you pray for me?" Why? They are always "right" in their own thinking. They are not immoral or wrong. If they went to a court of law, they might even come out winning. Their reasons are strong and their arguments sound.

Think about your own life—the way you acted with your parents, what you thought and what you did. Think of the cases you built against your authorities' decisions. Are you surprised? Don't be. Instead of simply obeying what God has asked us to do through our delegated authorities, we argue and try to reason things out in our heads. And we end up doing the same thing Eve did.

Don't misunderstand: I am not saying we should check our brains at the door and stop thinking. There are rare cases of abuse or clear disregard for God's authority in which we need to remove ourselves from under that authority or even disobey. But aside from those exceptional situations, the instruction is for us to come under the submission of God's authority by obeying those authorities God has placed over us. It means yielding even when our brain doesn't accept it or understand it. You see, the Word tells us that our natural mind is always at enmity with God, and it will not submit to Him.[7]

Mankind became independent from God, and the work of redemption brings us back to a place where we once again find our right and wrong in Him and not in ourselves. Second Corinthians 10:3–5 (NIV) gives us the instructions to handle these thoughts that plague us:

For though we live in the world, we do not wage war as the world does. The weapons we fight with [or warfare] are not the weapons of the world. On the contrary, they have divine power to demolish strongholds. We demolish arguments and every pretension that sets itself up against the knowledge of God, and we take captive every thought to make it obedient to Christ.

Then in Romans, Paul tells us:

Therefore, I urge you, brothers, in view of God's mercy, to offer your bodies as living sacrifices, holy and pleasing to God—this is your spiritual act of worship. Do not conform any longer to the pattern of this world, but be transformed by the renewing of your mind. Then you will be able to test and approve what God's will is—his good, pleasing and perfect will (Romans 12:1–2, NIV).

So now we come to the place where we can say, "God, I am open to You. Please help me." Otherwise we continue to rely on engaging our reason and walking in insubordination. But then who misses out? We do!

UNBROKENNESS AND PRIDE

As long as we believe we are someone extraordinarily important, we resist bending our necks. Often the incredibly competent are rebellious in their attitude. In Romans 12:3–5, Paul's exhortation to man is:

> For I say . . . to everyone who is among you, not to
> think of himself more highly than he ought to think,
> but to think soberly, as God has dealt to each one a
> measure of faith. For as we have many members in
> one body, but all the members do not have the same
> function, so we, being many, are one body in Christ,
> and individually members of one another.

For one reason or another, we can all have an elevated view of ourselves. The reasons are many—social status, fame, spiritual gifts, education, abilities, career position, spirituality, family background, experience, wealth and the list goes on. We start thinking about ourselves and become big in our own eyes. Samuel said of Saul, "You were *once* small in your own eyes" (1 Samuel 15:17, NIV, emphasis mine). But a day came when Saul saw himself as big and important, to the extent that he could make his own decisions. It was then that he rebelled against God's direction to him through Samuel, his spiritual delegated authority.

It sometimes happens like this with those who are given spiritual gifts. They may have only been walking with the Lord for a short while, whereas their pastor has been serving God for 25 or 30 years. But now they start getting the attention of the people, and they say to themselves, *Wow, my pastor can't do what I can, but I'm gifted by God.* They start looking down at their spiritual leader, and rebellion begins to grow in their hearts.

Obviously, these strengths or blessings are not evil in themselves. They are given by God. But being given much can put you on slippery ground if you're not careful. Submitting to authority means we take the place of a servant, but pride will not permit us to assume that place. So then pride and an unbending nature become the reason for rebellion.

Look at divorces, relationships that end in bitterness and juvenile delinquency cases, and you'll often find arrogant and stubborn people at the bottom of it. It's pride that responds, "I don't care what you say. I know better. Don't teach me! I am the captain of my soul, and I make my own decisions!" When pride has a hold on our lives, we can feel that we are "above" submitting to authority.

Naaman, the famous leper in the Old Testament, was the most powerful human being in Syria next to the king.[8] As commander of the army, when he walked through the streets his own people respected him and did whatever he commanded. But Naaman was full of leprosy.

He heard rumors about a mighty prophet in Israel and went there to get healed by Elisha. I am sure he expected an auspicious reception with a lot of gracious words being said to him. But now this strange prophet, who hardly had any riches and was living out in the middle of nowhere, sent out a servant boy to tell Naaman to go dip in the Jordan River seven times.

Naaman got mad and snapped, "I thought that he would surely come out to me and stand and call on the name of the LORD his God, wave his hand over the spot and cure me of my leprosy" (2 Kings 5:11, NIV). His anger grows, and he feels he has been treated disrespectfully. "What on earth is this two-bit prophet talking about? In my country we have rivers far better than the Jordan. Why can't I go there and be cleansed! What nonsense is this?"[9]

In his anger, Naaman starts to go back home. Why should he humble himself before this prophet who didn't even have the courtesy to come out and properly greet him? The truth is, to be healed Naaman had to submit to the one God had appointed to help him. He almost chose pride over healing. Then his servants said to him, "My father, if the prophet had told you to do some great thing, would you not have done it?" (2 Kings 5:13, NIV), and they pleaded with him to submit to what he had been told. Finally Naaman obeyed the instructions of Elisha.

What happened? He was healed, and his flesh was restored to that of a young boy. His pride and his own reasoning, however, had nearly kept him from the miracle he had been hoping for.

Look at Lucifer.[10] He was a beautiful cherub, immensely gifted and wise. But a time came when his gifts made him think he could ascend even higher, and he thought to himself, *I am important. I will exalt my throne above God's. Why should I submit to Him?*[11] And that's when he was cast down.

Today Satan is influencing people to follow his example. He encourages them to believe that because they are gifted, because they have wealth or because people respect their position, they too can plunge ahead and do as they think best.

INVICTUS

... I thank whatever gods may be
For my unconquerable soul.

In the fell clutch of circumstance
I have not winced nor cried aloud.
Under the bludgeonings of chance
My head is bloody, but unbowed.

... And yet the menace of the years
Finds, and shall find, me unafraid.

> It matters not how strait the gate,
> How charged with punishments the scroll,
> I am the master of my fate:
> I am the captain of my soul.[12]

Invictus means "unconquerable" in Latin. Those who follow this path become hard and proud, unconquerable. One man who was convicted of mass murder was convinced until the very end he was justified in his choices simply because he disagreed with his authority. He was executed and died proud and hard. He wrote the words of this poem by William Ernest Henley as his last words to this world.

Ezekiel 28:14 (NIV) says of Lucifer, "You *were* anointed as a guardian cherub, for so I ordained you" (emphasis mine). God did not take away his gifting and his abilities, his knowledge and his powers, but his anointing and his standing with God were gone. And he became Satan. The truth of the matter is that many times we can be more able in some way than our parents or pastor or teacher or boss or husband. But with that status alone, where do we end up?

Early in my life, I was given a little book called *The Calvary Road* by Roy Hession. In this volume was a small card, printed with the words, "Not 'I' but Christ." Interestingly, the *I* was drawn as a stubborn-looking man standing straight up. The *C* in *Christ* was a bent *I,* pictured as an individual with his head bowed, broken and humble.

When we look at Christ, we all become silent before His example:

Who, being in very nature God, did not consider equality with God something to be grasped, but made himself nothing, taking the very nature of a servant, being made in human likeness. And being found in appearance as a man, he humbled himself and became obedient to death—even death on a cross! (Philippians 2:6–8, NIV).

Let us be willing to allow God to change us into His likeness.

SCARS OF THE PAST

All of us have been treated unfairly. Without exception, we have suffered unkindness, misunderstandings and even abuse. This is the story of every human being. In a court we could probably prove that we have good reason to be bitter. Be careful, though! This bitterness can bring us to the place of speaking and acting against God's authority.

How do we go from someone else's careless actions against us to rebellion in our hearts? When our eyes are diseased, everything is foggy. In a similar fashion, unforgiveness turns into bitterness and affects our whole life. Our emotions, our minds and our wills are all contaminated and defiled.

In a sense it is like when we are physically ill. Our body is weak and run-down, and physically we can't do our normal work. The same is true in a spiritual sense. Bitterness wears down our spiritual immune system. Our insides get messed up, and we simply aren't capable of responding like someone who has a wholesome heart.

Most of the time, people don't even realize what has happened inside them. They fight and argue, unaware that a root of bitterness is causing this unrest in their soul. Nothing defiles a person of everything that is good like unforgiveness and bitterness. So it is that a heart affected by bitterness leads to rebellion and insubordination toward authorities.

The reason behind our bitterness may not necessarily have anything to do with an authority in our lives. It can be because of a co-worker, a brother or a sister. We can even manifest bitterness against God for some calamity that has happened.

Look at the older son in Luke 15.[13] A party was going on in the house for his younger brother. He knew he was expected to come, but he was angry and refused to attend. He was standing on the outside—not listening, not being sensitive to his authority. His spirit was shouting, "I am upset. What's happening is unjust." At last his father came out and pleaded with him to come inside. He still refused to listen to his father and spit out his hot words: "Look at this son of yours who wasted all your money. Why do you want to throw a party for him?"[14] Here was a man manifesting rebellion because he was bitter.

There are numerous stories like his. Unforgiveness distorts people's perception, and they easily become cynical toward their authority. Rebellion is simply the next step. Hebrews 12:15 warns us against this poison. It exhorts us to be diligent and guard against any root of bitterness growing within us. I cannot emphasize enough the importance of this verse.

When the offense has come from either a current or past authority figure, it makes obedience all the more difficult. We may have suffered under an ungracious or ungodly authority or experienced difficult circumstances with a delegated authority. We can walk away from a situation like this and move on, but often we carry with us that unforgiveness and anger toward authority. In any situation in which people experience difficulties with their given authority and do not forgive, it results in degrees of rebellion.

Sometimes in a church situation, people experience harshness or some kind of pain or disappointment related to church leadership. They leave that church and join another. They're thrilled and happy with everything at first. But in a short time, they get disgruntled, become critical and are no longer submissive to their pastor and elders. They never forgave their first pastor, and hence their underlying attitude has never changed. They still manifest an independent and rebellious spirit wherever they go.

Look at the children of Israel. They were always complaining and rebelling.[15] Could it be that because of the abusive authority they knew in Egypt, they viewed their new authorities with contempt as those who would also mistreat them like their slave masters had?

Think about this more, and you realize that for 400 years they had lived in Egypt under slavery. It's not too hard to imagine that many of these people developed anger and hatred toward authority. God had freed them from their bondage in Egypt as well as their abusive authority they had known there. They had the promises of God now before them. But how many of them carried that bitterness and unforgiveness out of the country with them? Then when trials and difficulties came, the children of Israel reacted in rebellion against Moses, the new authority God had placed over them.

There's a saying that a cat who falls into boiling water is scared even when it sees cold water. Once touched by scalding water, the animal fears any water, even though it's perfectly safe. It is reminded of the pain it suffered and doesn't want to risk that happening again!

When authority goes wrong, it is an incredibly hurtful situation for those who suffered under that influence. The devil uses these painful experiences, these scars from the past, to blind us from seeing the godly principle of submission. Those who have experienced abusive authority or very authoritative leadership, such as "Prophet's Movements" or Shepherding Movement theology, are like the cat who fell into the boiling water. Even remotely similar experiences remind them of the terrible distress they suffered. It is difficult for them to trust authority again because there was so much damage—ruined marriages, broken lives and brainwashing with Bible verses.

Wives who were abused in a previous marriage and are now married to a kind and gentle man may still have flashbacks and find it difficult to trust their new husband. It may take some time before they allow themselves to fully submit. Keen memories of the past can put up a defense mechanism because that's how she got through her last situation. Such extreme situations put fear in the back of one's head that says, "I don't want to go through that again." We shouldn't underestimate the difficulty such people have suffered.

Yet it is not beyond Christ to give the strength to forgive and to let Him heal those past scars. In spite of man's misuses of authority, God's foundation stays sure. He *can* restore us and help us learn to submit again and to experience hope and new life. It *is* better to walk afresh with God than to live in the memory of our past pain.

THE POWER OF INFLUENCE

People can have everything going for them. They can be humble of heart and without significant scars from the past. Yet they too can easily get swept into grave acts of rebellion. How? Through association with others. A significant reason for rebellion against authority is the negative influence of rebellious people.

When Lucifer fell, he was not alone. One-third of the angels followed him.[16] But take a moment to consider what they walked away from. They did not see spiritual matters dimly, like we do. Day and night these angels stood before God. They saw Him face-to-face. Not only that, until then they were living in a sinless state. They truly knew an awesome experience.

Yet great numbers of these angels were swayed by Lucifer and followed him. *How could that happen?*

It was the power of influence.

The power of influence is so strong that I see it as being one of the *main reasons* for church breakups, family breakups and the start of rebellions within organizations. I don't know how many have left my own movement for this very reason. This is a very dangerous cancer.

The story of Korah is a key example.[17] You remember what happened. Many of Israel's top leaders, who had seen God's wonderful acts, were influenced by Korah. By his influence, innocent people were swept away because they did not guard their hearts from his rebellion. Even today, how many innocent people have been wiped out because they were influenced by the wrong people and were blind to what was happening?

The rebellion began with Korah, just one person. In the end, however, 250 leaders and all the families of the three ringleaders were destroyed. Scripture warns us, "A little leaven leavens the whole lump" (1 Corinthians 5:6). In the early years of our seminary in India, I counseled my leaders and told them, "Work with the students no matter what they do. They will make mistakes. They're here to find help." But then I added, "There's one thing you should not tolerate—any form of rebellion. It is contagious." Stories of rebellions that began through the influence of one individual can be told time and again. They are all too common.

One such story is about a pastor and his congregation, which I knew for nearly two decades. There were more than 1,000 attending members, and every sign indicated this church was going to have a huge impact for the kingdom. There were many godly people involved, with a good man as their shepherd.

Then all of a sudden, like the erupting of a dormant volcano, problems surfaced. There was a tough split, and after a few years, less than 100 people made up the congregation. The tragedy the pastor and the church suffered began with one individual who reasoned in his head how things should be. He got disgruntled and became rebellious toward the church leadership. What began with one became "a group," and soon the damage was done.

The same misfortune happens in all walks of life. It invades politics. It appears in mission organizations. I've seen it happen within many ministries I know.

It should be obvious that these stories serve as a strong warning to us. When someone starts speaking negative things about those in authority, it should be like a siren in our hearts, screaming, "Be careful! Be careful! Be careful!"

The dilemma is that it can be an assistant pastor, a worship leader, an elder, a deacon or a well-respected person who leads the innocent sheep into this rebellion against their delegated authority. The insubordination within that 1,000-member church had everything to do with the influence of one significant assistant leader.

Look at the 10 elders in Israel who gave evil reports to the people.[18] The 10 were all top leaders. They were as gifted as Joshua and Caleb to lead the people of God. Nevertheless, it was through their influence that unbelief and rebellion were instigated against Moses—their delegated authority.

I know a leader who worked with an organization. He was given all the freedom in the world to work with everyone. But he actually started influencing some of these individuals to rebel against their leadership and, in the end, walk away from the ministry. These innocent people were not mature enough to understand that from the time he started to demonstrate insubordination, he was not acting in a godly manner—that he was not someone whom they should follow. They trusted him completely and did not guard their hearts. In the end, they followed after him.

It can all begin so innocently. One person may say a few things in a private prayer meeting like, "I am concerned about our leader. He is a godly brother. He works hard. We love him and his family. What sacrifices he has made for God. . . ." Then, under the cover of concern and prayer requests, all kinds of negative innuendos are made about his authority. Before you know it, emails are sent, phone calls are made and everything gets carried to the next level. That little "prayer concern" eventually becomes the poison that destroys many lives.

It can happen innocently among young people who have mentors they love and respect. But they take for granted that their thoughts are right and don't realize they are criticizing those in authority.

It can even be a senior leader speaking ill of an associate under him to one of this man's own people. This person can think, *Wow, the big boss says that about my leader. Why do I have to listen to him? He obviously doesn't know what he's doing.*

How many children have grown up in godly homes but fall prey to bad habits because of the rebellious influence of new-found friends in college or university where they attend?

Even a casual conversation with a co-worker, discussing shared hurts related to a leader, can be the start of incredible damage in the work of God.

Guarding our hearts against anything that causes insubordination or a lack of respect toward authority should be taken very seriously. God warns us to have nothing to do with those who sow discord among the brethren—not even sharing meals with them.[19]

Masses were led astray because they did not protect their ears from Absalom's deceiving words. Possibly millions of angels didn't have to lose their privileges forever and be cast out of heaven had they chosen not to be influenced by Lucifer. They could have said, "We have seen God, the Creator, and we are not going to rebel against Him."

So it is today; we still have that choice. When it comes to our friends, our fellowship with others, we need to be incredibly careful. If someone you look up to manifests rebellion toward authority, don't join him or her in their sin.

One time someone told me of his frustration with a leader. I asked him why he felt this way. I found out that this individual had no personal interaction at all with this leader. However, his close friend had great difficulty with him, and through their conversations, this innocent man was now unhappy and critical toward this Christian leader.

If you are seeking counsel, please find people who know God. Don't gravitate toward those who agree with everything you think and say. They are not the kind of friends to help you. Find people who are not afraid to tell you, "You are wrong. This is not the way to do it." They will teach you the ways of the Lord. They will not aid your heart in acts of rebellion.

Then guard your heart from being influenced by the words and actions of others so that you are not marked by rebellion. Be cautious about allowing yourself to listen to television programs or movies that foster rebellion. When you sense the spirit of someone is critical, protect your heart from their words, lest you become defiled. If you happen to hear such evil talk, say quietly in your heart something like this: "In Jesus' name I reject these words. I do not receive them."

If it is a leader who is promoting insubordination against authority, be careful not to join in the ranks.

Any of us can easily fall prey to the negative influence of others if we don't purpose to guard our hearts against it.

FOR THE LACK OF FAITH THERE IS REBELLION

Our submission to authority rests on faith. Likewise, our rebellion stems from a lack of faith. More than we realize, we live with rebellion in our hearts because of our unwillingness to believe God's Word and act on it.

Often it is our human logic that stops us from trusting God to see us through. Faith is not counter to logic or reason; it is beyond it. Imagine with me this possible conversation between God and Noah:

God calls, "Hi, Noah!"

"Yes, God!" he responds.

"I want you to build an ark."

"What did you say?" Noah responds.

"A boat. A building that floats on the water. This is how I want you to build it. . . ."

God gives Noah all the instructions for this project. I am sure Noah agonized over this rather unusual idea. It probably made no sense to him. I can see Noah's son observing his dilemma and saying, "Daddy, what's happened?"

"Son, I just can't figure this out. God told me that there is going to be a flood, and we need to build an ark."

"What are you talking about? There's going to be a flood? There's going to be rain? Not even a drop of water has ever come down from the sky! That makes no sense."

Can you just imagine Noah trying in his mind to figure this out?

Noah probably hired carpenters. I can see them out working with their chisels and hammers, saying to each other, "Man, what exactly are we doing?"

"What do you mean? We're building a boat."

"But for what?"

"Oh, the old man is cracked."

"It doesn't matter; we're getting our money! Just keep on building it!"

The project made no logical sense. But the Bible says, "Noah did everything just as God commanded him."[20] Through his obedience, Noah touched godliness.

What was the secret of David's life of submission in the midst of such incredible pain and suffering? His own testimony declares: "I had fainted, unless I had *believed* to see the goodness of the LORD in the land of the living" (Psalm 27:13, KJV, emphasis mine).

It is our lack of faith that urges us to rebel and act independently. When we are faced with adverse circumstances or when the authorities over us make poor decisions, we must choose to believe in the sovereignty of God[21] instead of our human reasoning. We trust in God to make everything right in the end.[22] If we choose not to believe in Him, we will lean upon our own understanding, and we will soon end up fighting for our personal rights.

Hagar had the courage to go back and submit to her unkind authority because she had faith in God's promise to her.[23] If she sought to live by sight and logic, she would never have made that choice.

If we believe that God's Word is true and that He will protect us and grow us in godliness and bless us when we obey the authorities He appointed, then we don't have to understand or agree with everything our authorities do in order to be submissive. We can believe that in spite of our hurts from the past, God's promises remain true.[24] And He will bless our obedience even when it doesn't make sense.

We must begin to see beyond our delegated authority to the God who placed us under those people. If we choose to look beyond, we will not just see the man or woman in authority over us, but the sacredness of "authority" God has established and His unlimited power to make things right in the end.

The author of rebellion, Satan, will continue to use unbelief to try to keep us under his influence. Don't forget that "unbelief" was the weapon he used to cause Eve to rebel against God and Adam, her delegated authority.

But God is forever restoring what Satan destroyed. We can choose to say, "Father, not my will, but Your will be done." When we come to that place of total surrender, we can honestly say, "I am not going to attempt to be so smart about this. I will not protect my interests any longer. I choose to stop fighting."

It is now through faith in Christ that we are a new creation. Let us learn to live with submission, trusting in God's Word, so that in the end it will be well with us.

Lord, thank You for Your grace toward us and Your words of promise. Please meet with us. Take these truths and touch us deeply in our souls as only You can do. Teach us to walk with You as You desire. Lord, we trust You to help us on this journey. We cannot do this on our own. Thank You for everything. Amen.

Study Guide for Chapter 8 begins on page 246.

NINE

BIBLICAL PRINCIPLES FOR EXERCISING AUTHORITY

Why do we spend money to buy an umbrella? The answer is simple. During the rainy season, we want to be protected from the driving rain. In the summer when it's blistering hot, we want protection from the heat. Similarly, delegated authority is God's appointed protection for the people under them.

But suppose there are holes in the umbrella—it can't protect those under it. When the umbrella (authority) doesn't function any longer, all those who should be protected get rained on, scorched, humiliated and injured. All who are in authority should consider how sobering their responsibility is.

David sinned by numbering his fighting men.[1] Joab, his right-hand man, said, "Oh, my lord! With little or much we get along fine. God is with us! What makes you want to go and figure out how strong you are? Please don't do this" (2 Samuel 24:3, paraphrased). But David wouldn't listen.

Then the judgment of God fell. Why? Because of this leader's sin. And who got hurt? Not just David, but thousands of innocent people.

Although many suffer when there is ungodly authority, ultimately it is those in authority who are held responsible for their stewardship of the people God has entrusted to them. Thus, requirement for those in authority is more severe than we may want to acknowledge.

Let me remind you that to some degree, all of us are in authority. If you are an older brother, you are partially responsible for your younger sisters and brothers. If you are a father, you are responsible for your wife and your children. If your parents are dead and you have siblings under you, according to the Bible you are the one responsible. If you are an older sister in the local church, the Bible says you should instruct the younger ones.[2]

However, only the one who is under authority himself can be an authority, for all authority comes from God. No matter what position or title we have, we must live with the awareness that each of us is under authority.

My responsibility is that of a leader over a movement with several thousand pastors and Christian workers in many nations. Yet I am not without authorities over me. I am under a number of delegated authorities in my life.

In my culture, when my father died, my mother became the authority. When my mother passed away, my oldest brother assumed that role.

I remember one time I went to my village on a return visit from the United States. My oldest brother and I started talking, and he said something that upset me. I even began arguing with him. He raised his voice and said, "You think you know everything. But remember, I represent our father." I knew exactly what he meant.

I was angry. I got in the car, and my driver drove off. We traveled from my home in Niranam to a place called Kadapra (about three kilometers away). As we came to the intersection where we would next turn toward the airport to catch my flight to Europe, I suddenly told the driver, "Turn around."

"Turn around?" he asked. "Where are we going?"

"Back home," I said.

We quickly returned to the place where the earlier argument had taken place. I looked out and saw my brother still there. The first statement he said was, "I knew you would come back."

He was right. During those three kilometers I had said to myself, *What have I done?* I got out of the car and hugged my brother. I said, "Please forgive me. I am so sorry," and he cried.

Then he said, "Let me pray for you." And he did. Then I got back in the car and headed again toward the airport. Being in a significant leadership position in my world didn't release me from respecting the authority of my eldest brother.

Look around and you can quickly see the families, churches, businesses, communities and nations that are destroyed because of the sins of those in authority. Adolf Hitler is only one recent example of how a great nation can be destroyed by one individual in authority.

Think about Eli the priest, who failed to give leadership to his sons and had to hear about them dying an untimely death at the hand of God.[3]

I can think of churches and ministries damaged due to sin and unwise decisions made by a pastor or leader. I'm sure you know a number of similar situations.

It is with this sobering reality in mind that we next search the Scriptures as to what the Lord's desire is for those He has placed in leadership.

AUTHORITY COMES FROM GOD

Romans 13:1 tells us, "Let every soul be subject to the governing authorities. For there is no authority except *from God,* and the authorities that exist are appointed by God" (emphasis mine). We are not *the Authority.* God alone is *the Authority.* All authority is appointed and directed by Him.

When this perspective is fully understood and applied, it will transform any leader. It is incredibly important for us to remember that the basis for our authority is not appointment by man, our title or our own power but rather the fact that God Almighty set us in that position. When we forget this, we assume God's position of authority and are actually seeking to sit on His throne!

King Nebuchadnezzar did this very thing.[4] He was the mighty king of ancient Babylon. His city was a wonder of the world, unmatched by anything else. Who hasn't heard of the Hanging Gardens of Babylon? He was truly an amazing man. Yet he only had authority based on the fact that God, the Almighty, gave it to him.

One day Nebuchadnezzar had a dream. The prophet Daniel told the king its meaning: "You will be driven away from people and will live with the wild animals; you will eat grass like cattle and be drenched with the dew of heaven. Seven times will pass by for you until you acknowledge that the Most High is sovereign over the kingdoms of men and gives them to anyone he wishes" (Daniel 4:25, NIV).

Twelve months later, the ruler's dream became reality. We read about the king boasting, "Is not this the great Babylon I have built as the royal residence, by my mighty power and for the glory of my majesty?" (Daniel 4:30, NIV). Then even as the words were barely out of his mouth, a voice came from heaven, saying,

> "This is what is decreed for you, King Nebuchadnezzar:
> Your royal authority has been taken from you. You will
> be driven away from people and will live with the wild
> animals; you will eat grass like cattle. Seven times will
> pass by for you until you acknowledge that the Most
> High is sovereign over the kingdoms of men and gives
> them to anyone he wishes" (Daniel 4:31–32, NIV).

What had been foretold was fulfilled. Nebuchadnezzar was driven away from people and ate grass like cattle. He remained in that confused state for the allotted time.

Then at the end of that season of learning, Nebuchadnezzar says:

> "I . . . raised my eyes toward heaven, and my sanity was
> restored. Then I praised the Most High; I honored
> and glorified him who lives forever. His dominion

is an eternal dominion; his kingdom endures from
generation to generation. All the peoples of the earth
are regarded as nothing. He does as he pleases with
the powers of heaven and the peoples of the earth"
(Daniel 4:34–35, NIV).

His lesson learned, King Nebuchadnezzar's sanity was restored.
What a sobering story.

It shows us how serious an affront it is to the Lord when we
assume His authority. Whatever position we are in, it is God who
put us there. He can just as easily remove us.

Civil servants, police, judges and the like enforce the laws, but
they don't make them. Laws are made by a higher authority. In
the same way, as someone in authority, we are only responsible to
execute what the Lord has given us to do.

A few years ago, I flew into the Frankfurt International Airport in Germany, planning to take a domestic flight to Berlin. I
gave my passport to the immigration officer, and he started to flip
through it. I wondered to myself, *What is he looking for?*

"Where is your visa?" he asked.

"I don't need a visa," I replied. "Can't you see how many stamps
I have in my passport? I have been here plenty of times."

He looked at me and explained, "They changed the law. Didn't
you hear? Indians are now required to have a visa to get into
Germany."

I pulled out my air tickets and said, "But look at this. I have to
go to Berlin. I have a meeting. They are waiting for me." He listened to my whole desperate speech. But in the end he just made
this statement, "Sir, I don't make the laws. I only execute them."

As we realize this, it will help us be humble leaders. We are not God. We are only His delegated authority. If people under us don't obey us, they are really responding to the Lord in rebellion. It is His job to take care of it. We don't have to feel guilty and try to make anything happen. This gives us great relief.

LEAD BY EXAMPLE

An ambassador to another country carries the responsibility and weight of properly representing his or her homeland. Everything communicated and done is received as a reflection of the policies, beliefs and wishes of the government. This is a heavy responsibility, and failure to accurately represent his or her country is a serious matter.

Now, as a delegated authority of Almighty God, think how serious our responsibility is. What we say, what we do and how we take care of those He has entrusted to us are a reflection on Him.

Writing to the seven churches in the book of Revelation, Christ *did not* address His warnings to the congregations. Rather, He addressed them to the pastor of the church.

Looking back on ecclesiastical history, there is a direct correlation between the Dark Ages of the Church and the times those in authority greatly misrepresented their Lord. Think of the Inquisition, even the Crusades, and the thousands murdered by the Church in the name of God. These leaders were blind and deaf to the living God. When those in authority go wrong, everything goes haywire.

Read through 1 and 2 Kings, and you'll quickly see how God's people suffered when their leaders went wrong.[5]

The truth is, people often suffer because of their leaders. At the same time, all leaders are responsible to God for those He has entrusted to them: "[Your spiritual leaders'] work is to watch over your souls, and they are accountable to God" (Hebrews 13:17, NLT). So who must fear the most? Not the people. Rather, the one in authority must serve the Lord, understanding the grave seriousness of his or her responsibility.

Godliness and proven character are supremely important for all leaders. Unless we maintain close fellowship with God through the Word, prayer and fasting, how will we properly represent *the Authority*? How will we know what instructions He is giving us? How will we know how to exercise authority over the people and the work God has appointed to us?

If Jesus needed to stay in such close contact with God that He could say He only did what His Father showed Him to do, how much more do we need the same? How can we assume that we can get by even for a moment without involving the Father, if Jesus could not? If He desperately needed the Father's input, don't we even more so need to hear from the Lord in all we do?

As leaders, we need to be people who can be watched and followed. In 1 Corinthians Paul says, "Follow my example, as I follow the example of Christ" (11:1, NIV). He didn't say, "Follow me. I have knowledge." No. He simply said, "Follow me—my life, the example you have seen in me as I have followed Christ." As we follow Christ closely, others should then be able to follow us.

But how can you and I be an example to those we lead unless our hearts are right before God and man? Without honesty and integrity in our dealings, how can we possibly represent the living Lord?

Don't let the wall around your family, your ministry or whatever the realm of your responsibility be broken down through your anger, bitterness, greed, lust or other sins. Don't be like the leaders from church history or in the Old Testament accounts who led their people into darkness. May God help us fear Him, knowing we will be held accountable for all those He has put in our care.

PICK UP YOUR CROSS

A godly authority is someone who walks a narrow road—daily choosing to die to self. It is not possible to function as a godly authority without self-denial, for often we must die to our own desires in order to carry out His assignments.

Galatians 2:20 should be true in our lives: "I have been crucified with Christ; it is no longer I who live, but Christ lives in me." When strong-willed individuals are in authority, they have a tendency of getting in the way of representing God and being a leader who builds others. Like King Saul, though they remain in a position of leadership, their effectiveness is gone. Their focus is not on the Lord, but rather on themselves.

There may be some who believe that being in authority will make their lives easier. Nothing could be further from the truth. As a matter of fact, being a good leader means working more, praying more, fasting more, suffering more and facing more misunderstandings. It is the parents who fast and pray desperately for their children. A godly leader is one who often deliberately chooses inconveniences to lead the people God has entrusted to him or her. It is not one who says, "How can I have an easier life, gain more recognition and have others as my servants?"

Few will follow you unless you show the way and also accept inconveniences. Paul illustrates this so well when he writes about his life among the Ephesians:

> I have not coveted anyone's silver or gold or clothing. You yourselves know that these hands of mine have supplied my own needs and the needs of my companions. In everything I did, I showed you that by this kind of hard work we must help the weak, remembering the words the Lord Jesus himself said: "It is more blessed to give than to receive" (Acts 20:33–35, NIV).

Ultimately it means that we need to come to a place of complete surrender. We are not representing ourselves. We are not leading for our own benefit. Our life is Christ's, and what we do is for Him. To be a godly leader, our life must be surrendered to Him.

Surrender is submission. It is being someone who is not fighting for themselves, but is seeking to hear and obey the Lord. It means not only submitting to Him, but often submitting to one another as circumstances dictate.

To be in authority does not mean you no longer need to submit to others. Obviously there are always going to be people we are either responsible to or are elder to us. A heart that is surrendered does not resist these opportunities. Our flesh hates it, but there is a peace and rest that come only when our hearts are surrendered.

A few years ago, I was on the phone with George Verwer. He is the founder of Operation Mobilization, a worldwide movement, and one of the godliest individuals I know. He became my leader when I was barely 17 and joined Operation Mobilization. To this day I still consider him as my mentor.

During this conversation, George, unlike his normal character, said something that hurt me. I was caught by surprise. "George, listen," I said. Then I talked back to him. I argued, saying something like, "Look, I'm sorry you are blaming me for this, but it is your people who are at fault."

He said, "Oh, I am so sorry. I should have been more careful with my words." The conversation went on, and we finished our discussion. I hung up the telephone.

But then I sat there in my office looking at the telephone. "What have I done?" I asked myself. I got scared. I had argued with George Verwer, which I never could have imagined doing! I picked up the telephone and called him back.

"Hello," he said.

"Um," I said, trying to hold back my emotions.

Again he said, "Hello," but I couldn't talk.

"Hello?"

I said, "George, it's me. I am calling to ask you to forgive me." There was silence. I continued, "I should never have talked to you like I did."

I remember so clearly his next statement: "No wonder God has raised you up to such a position as this. Can I pray with you?"

I said yes. He prayed and blessed me and then hung up.

I didn't want to call. It was difficult for me to do. Picking up our cross is always a choice between our own way and the Lord's way.

Thomas à Kempis, a monk from the 14th century, said, "Carry the cross patiently, and with perfect submission; and in the end it shall carry you."[6] That is the way of surrender. In surrender we can be confident that the Lord will take care of the outcome and will cause our lives to bear much fruit.

HUMILITY IS A MUST

Roy Hession says, "Humility, lamb-likeness, the surrender of our wills to God, are what He looks for supremely from man."[7]

When Jesus described Himself, the words He chose were "gentle and humble."[8] We, as His delegated authority, can only rightly represent Him if we too are humble. Humility is knowing who we are in light of who God is. The more we comprehend who God truly is, the more humble we become.

You are in authority. You are a leader. You are intelligent. You have an education. You have a good income. Which of these did you not receive as a gift from God? If we compare ourselves to others, we can become proud. If we look at these assets in light of God Himself, what do they even matter?

Humility will sustain us, whereas pride will always hurt our authority. King Uzziah was only 16 when he became king.[9] He did not know how to rule. This young man asked God for help, and He blessed him and stood by him. Uzziah became a mighty king. Then we read this sad verse: "When he was strong his heart was lifted up, to his destruction" (2 Chronicles 26:16). When his story ends, we read that the king was confined to a leper colony. Pride, or lack of humility, was the reason for his fall. Uzziah forgot that it was God who blessed him and made him a successful delegated authority, not his own greatness.

Some may say in their hearts, "Don't teach me. I know what I am doing! I don't need to ask anybody for help."

But the Lord says, "How sad. Don't you see? You are naked. You are blind." He then extends an invitation, "Walk away from all this. Come to Me, and I will restore your eyesight. But you have to admit that you are blind."[10]

Here is a strange truth: The moment we think we are better than someone else, we have violated this principle of authority, and humility is shattered. Consider others better than yourself. Now who said that? God did (see Philippians 2:3).

Often those in leadership fear that if they admit their sins, people will think less of them. The truth is that we are all failing people, and we will do wrong. Humility leads us to become godly authorities through admitting our failures. Even Paul, after 20 years of preaching, said that he was the chief of sinners.[11] Who are we then? Why not be honest with people so they can say, "How interesting. He sometimes fails too. I have hope."

C.S. Lewis writes:

> Do not imagine that if you meet a really humble man he will be what most people call "humble" nowadays: he will not be a . . . person, who is always telling you that . . . he is nobody. Probably all you will think about him is that he seemed a cheerful, intelligent chap who took a real interest in what *you* said to *him*. . . . He will not be thinking about humility: he will not be thinking about himself at all.[12]

True humility transforms you from within so whatever you do has its flavoring. Every aspect of being an authority stems from our humility or our lack of it.

WITHOUT FORCE

Peter addresses the leaders of the church in 1 Peter:

> Therefore, I exhort the elders among you, as your
> fellow elder and witness of the sufferings of Christ,
> and a partaker also of the glory that is to be revealed,
> shepherd the flock of God among you, exercising
> oversight not under compulsion, but voluntarily,
> according to the will of God; and not for sordid gain,
> but with eagerness; nor yet as lording it over those
> allotted to your charge, but proving to be examples
> to the flock (1 Peter 5:1–3, NASB).

What does it mean to "lord it over"? The Oxford Dictionary defines this as "act in a superior and domineering manner."[13]
Domineering is defined this way: "showing a desire or tendency
to exercise excessive control or authority over others."[14]

God gave mankind free will. He does not *force* us to do anything. When we attempt as leaders to force obedience through
manipulation of any kind, the Lord has no part in it, and we are
not representing Him and His character.

There are various ways leaders manipulate people into obedience. Some use fear tactics to lord it over others. Sad to say, inse-
cure leaders stoop to verbal abuse so they can remain in control
of their people. We cannot forget the religious fundamentalists
who brainwash the masses.

The abuse of power is devastatingly destructive—and yet so
common. A cursory observation of cults is sufficient to convince
anyone of this painful reality. The Shepherding Movement's the-

ology destroyed many lives through its pyramid structure and fear of being ostracized. With authoritative governments, we see the suffering of the masses who live in total fear. Whether it is an authority in the home, church, workplace or nation, innocent people are too frequently abused by leaders who are more concerned with being "in control" than taking care of their people. Whenever human dignity is violated and freedom is removed from the picture, authority is no longer biblical or beneficial.[15]

I remember talking to a Christian woman, a wife and mother of four children, who shared her pain and asked for prayer. "My husband is a good man," she said. "He doesn't abuse me physically, but from the first day of our marriage, he has abused me verbally. No matter what I say, he tells me, 'You don't know anything. You are to obey me and do what I tell you.' " She tried to share her heart with him about many things, but nothing worked. Finally she gave up.

Before her marriage, she was joyful and active in the Lord's work. But now she is not allowed to do anything beyond her responsibilities as a wife and mother. She talked to her husband about the growing number of children they have. He would not listen to her. Though her health was poor, he insisted on having as many children as possible. She confided, "I died on the inside. I feel I am just a cook and a machine to produce offspring for him."

Then she told me, "I love my husband, but I suffer greatly and often cry myself to sleep."

This marriage is a case of abused authority. Her sad story is an example of an authority who is not concerned about representing the heart of the Lord in caring for those under him.

Watchman Nee says, "But one who has been dealt with by

God has a special characteristic. He is not one to be unfaithful or to keep silent; he is faithful and he speaks, but he never forces people to accept his thought."[16] May this be our heart as we serve those under us.

THE SERVANT OF ALL

The Bible states that those who desire to be in a position of leadership desire a good thing.[17] When the disciples argued among themselves about who was the greatest, Jesus didn't say, "You crazy people. Don't try to be great; you should try to be nothing and do nothing." No, He made it clear: "If anyone desires to be first, he shall be last of all and servant of all" (Mark 9:35).

Following the passage in which Jesus instructs them not to lord it over others like the Gentiles do, He closes by telling the disciples, "For even the Son of Man did not come to be served, but to serve, and to give His life a ransom for many" (Mark 10:45). If Christ, being God, chose to lead by serving rather than being served, how much more should we lead those placed under us by being a servant?

Hours before going to the cross, Jesus chose to leave His disciples with an example He wanted them to follow.[18] In the middle of their last supper together, Jesus got up, laid aside His clothes and put a towel around His waist. He then went to each disciple, bent down and washed his feet.

Once He finished, He asked the Twelve, "Do you know what I have done to you?" (John 13:12). Then He went on to say, "If I then, your Lord and Teacher, have washed your feet, you also ought to wash one another's feet. For I have given you an example, that you should do as I have done to you" (John 13:14–15).

This is the image Jesus wanted to leave with His followers—a leader who does not act superior to anyone but who looks for opportunities to serve and, even more so, to serve those he is responsible for. Jesus is our example. He shows us the way.

When we serve the Lord with humility, it means we are actively looking for ways to minister to others as their servant. Jesus concludes His object lesson by telling the disciples, "If you know these things, you are blessed if you do them" (John 13:17, NASB).

GOVERN WITH LOVE AND GRACE

Just before Jesus challenged His disciples with His final example of being a servant, it says in John 13:1 (NIV), "Having loved his own who were in the world, he now showed them the full extent of his love." Love is the track on which being a servant rides. There can be outward manifestations of being a servant, but these will only last so long before attitudes turn bitter, if the service is not done out of love.

Ephesians 5:25 says, "Husbands, love your wives, just as Christ also loved the church and gave Himself for her." The Lord wants us to love those He has given us to be responsible for, to consider and care for them. Love and grace must always govern our judgments, decisions and ways of dealing with people when we are in a position of authority.

As I look back over my leadership in the work of God, one of my regrets is how I sometimes dealt with people. Although it was not deliberate, often my unkind words, quick decisions and harshness hurt people. Because I am in leadership, people don't often express their feelings, and many times I did not recognize what I had done. But they suffered. I wish I could go back and correct all these mistakes. All I can say now is, "Lord, forgive me. I want to learn."

I have an instruction that I give to my people in leadership: I tell them to err on the side of grace and love, not on the side of legalism and being right. We should be fighting for our people to succeed and going out of our way to help them do better. Love covers a multitude of sins and maintains the dignity of others. D.E. Hoste[19] said of Hudson Taylor, "The high standard of self-sacrifice and toil which he ever kept before himself, never made him lacking in tenderness and sympathy toward those who were not able to go as far as he did in these respects."[20]

If God were to deal with me based on whether I did everything right, I would have been dead long ago. If it were not for the grace and mercy of God, none of us would still be alive. So much has been granted to us by a merciful God—how much more, then, should we in turn be gracious?

The parable of the lost son, in Luke 15, is a picture of God's gracious heart.[21] Obviously the younger son was in rebellion, and his father must have rightfully asked, "Why, my son?"

The son just said, "Just give me my share." So his father gave it to him, and the son walked away.

It's my conviction that it took a greater love for the father to let his son go than to hold him back. Love gives freedom. Love allows people the room to make choices.

THE LORD'S SERVANT MUST NOT STRIVE

In the past, I struggled with people, trying to make them understand, to make them change. I pleaded with them and cried for them. I prayed with them and for them. I used to live with such frustration, agony and even anger. I would say, "When will they ever learn? When will they understand?"

Then one day the Lord spoke to my heart, "My servant should not strive. Don't fight. Let it be. I called you to speak on My behalf. Invite people to respond. You are not the authority. I am the One in control. Just be My servant."

You can't imagine the peace that filled my heart when I finally gave up trying to change anyone.

There will be times of rebellion, even slander and insubordination, from those we oversee. These are not easy times, but our response is ever so critical. God is watching how we handle it.

Moses faced a great deal of opposition from the people he led, yet he did not fight for their respect or his position.[22] In fact, he would go to God on their behalf, begging Him not to kill them.[23] We need to learn from his example.

Those in authority should never fight for themselves. We need to simply leave it to the Lord to defend us. He will do a much better job in His time and His way than we ever could. In fact, when a leader fights to establish his authority, he actually loses his ability to lead.[24]

When the Corinthians attacked Paul, he didn't fight back. Rather, with love and kindness, he exhorted them as a loving father would. His care for them comes through so clearly in the book of 2 Corinthians.[25] This is the way of peace that the Lord wants us to walk in as leaders. Paul told Timothy, "And the servant of the Lord must not strive" (2 Timothy 2:24, KJV). This truth has set me free more times than I can say. May it also set you free—free to let God be God and simply to follow Him.

DO NOT MISUSE AUTHORITY

Authority and responsibility should never be a license to do what we want. When we do so, we misrepresent God and misuse our authority.

For 30 long years, Moses led the children of Israel. How he suffered in this role. He had to put up with a great deal of complaining. How often he must have prayed and cried out for these multitudes. He paid a heavy price to lead these obstinate people. God called him the meekest man on earth.[26] He also said of Moses, "To others I speak in visions and dreams and riddles, but to Moses I speak face to face" (Numbers 12:6–8, paraphrased).

For three decades Moses suffered and loved and had patience with these people. But finally, he was tired of it all, and he got upset. God said, "Moses, just speak to the rock. Water will come out."[27] But out of frustration and anger, instead of just speaking—he struck the rock.

In doing this, he misrepresented the Lord before the people. And Moses, the delegated authority, was punished severely for his actions.

We can wonder, "Didn't God see what these people did to Moses? What rebellion! What ungodliness! Couldn't He have taken that into consideration?" While He was angry with Moses,

God never said a word against the congregation in this case. But to Moses, the delegated authority, He took him aside and said, "You cannot enter the Promised Land."[28]

When God places us in a position of authority and we violate our responsibility, becoming careless and representing God in a way we should not—He may quickly forgive a million people of their complaining, but His delegated authority He holds accountable and reprimands severely. There are serious consequences for misusing authority.

HOW THEN SHALL WE BE?

In the battle with the Amalekites, King Saul chose to fear the people more than he feared the Lord. At the end of the conversation with Samuel, Saul said, "I have sinned. But please honor me before the elders of my people and before Israel; come back with me" (1 Samuel 15:30, NIV). As leaders, we have a natural tendency to want to appear competent before others. There is a fear that if they don't respect us, if they see our faults, they will not follow us. But the Word of God tells us that before honor is humility. Saul tried to take an easier way for the flesh. He chose honor first instead of humility, and he lost everything.

A godly leader is one who is more concerned about following the Lord's direction than catering to what the people might think. Matthew 23:11–12 (NASB) says, "But the greatest among you shall be your servant. Whoever exalts himself shall be humbled; and whoever humbles himself shall be exalted." If, like Saul, we try to honor ourselves, we will be humbled. But if we choose the way of humility, in time we will be exalted and honored.

This heart of submission represents the fruit of all the traits of a godly leader. You would do well to take time to think about this.

I have had my own struggles in this area. My board made a decision at one point that they wanted to increase my salary. It was an expression of their love and kindness. They said, "We have decided that this is how much you should now receive." But my wife and I were happy with what we were already getting. God blessed our children, and they are healthy. What else could we want? We have a nice house, and I have the best car in the whole universe, a 1962 Volkswagen Bug. It's 46 years old, but it runs like a top. I was happy.

I told the people at the office, "When you make out my allowance, just give me the same amount I always take. I don't want any more." And the people in our finance office followed my instructions.

With another board meeting coming up later, our business manager said to me, "May I tell you something? If you do not listen to these men to whom you are accountable and do not take the money they told you to take, how can they believe that you will listen to them in other matters? What will they think when they find out you are not accepting the raise they told you to take?"

These godly board members wanted to bless me, but I just wanted my needs met. For the first time it dawned on me that these people I was accountable to had made a decision, and by not taking the money, I was in rebellion. I was overcome with fear.

During the next board meeting I told the board, "I need to ask you for forgiveness for something I have done. I have violated the authority God placed over me. I hope you will have mercy toward me and be willing to forgive me for having done wrong." And there was dead silence because they had no idea what I was going to say.

I continued, "You decided that I should take this amount of money. But my wife and I, we have no need for it. We just want to meet our needs, and so I didn't take it. I recognize now that I was not submitting to the authority God placed in my life." By this point I was crying. I said, "I just want you to forgive me. I don't know what else I can tell you."

One of the senior board members said, "Well, when we made that decision, we gave you the permission to take it or not. So we release you." It was like a wonderful cool shower in the summertime when I heard that. Then everybody said of my decision, "That is fine."

For me, this experience came down to the questions: Do I, as a leader, submit to the authority God has placed in my life? and Do I take such opportunities given to me to submit? I am learning too.

In the end, we find that God's view of a leader is quite different from what we may think on the surface. Roy Lessin's poem "A Godly Leader" puts it well:

> A Godly leader . . .
> finds strength by realizing his weakness,
> finds authority by being under authority,
> finds direction by laying down his own plans,
> finds vision by seeing the needs of others,
> finds credibility by being an example,

finds loyalty by expressing compassion,
finds honor by being faithful,
finds greatness by being a servant.[29]

As we look at what the Lord expects from us as leaders, I'm sure we all fall short. I know I do. But I'm grateful for the lessons I am learning and the deep responsibility I feel for the beautiful people God has placed under my authority. Don't be discouraged. There's a season to sow and a season to reap. As you receive the Word of God, it will bring forth fruit that will glorify Him and bless your life.

Lord, thank You for Your mercy. How fragile and weak we are. We seem to continually fall under deception—our Enemy is active and alive. We pray that You will help us become a peculiar people that will follow You all the days of our lives—humble, simple, broken, unassuming disciples of the Lamb of God. Dear Lord, this is Your kingdom. Grant us understanding, we pray. Amen.

Study Guide for Chapter 9 begins on page 249.

TEN

WHEN OUR AUTHORITIES
GO WRONG

By the very title of this chapter, it is obvious that there will be occasions when authorities over us make wrong choices. Please note, I did not say *the* Authority, which is God. I am referring to delegated human authorities: a king, a boss at work, a prime minister, a husband, a judge, a parent or a pastor.

After all we have studied, there can be no doubt that God desires us to have a submissive heart, and He seeks to bless those who honor their authorities. Yet how does God want us to respond when we are faced with hard and difficult circumstances concerning our authorities? What are we supposed to do when they misuse and even abuse their powers? Is there a time and a place to resist authority? If so, how do we respond without being defiled by the spirit of rebellion?

There are definitely times when we need to express our concerns to our leaders. Sometimes we need to remove ourselves from under their authority. Unfortunately, there are also situations when we must even disobey our delegated authority.

These are not easy issues. Please be warned that we are entering a dangerous zone. Unless we are careful, we can allow our own reasoning in these situations to lead us into rebellious responses. We must earnestly guard our heart and make certain we are not looking for excuses to disobey based on our own self-centeredness and subjective reasoning.

Making the right choice comes down to having a heart of submission and sincerely seeking to hear what the Lord is saying to us in these specific situations. There are no pre-fabricated, black-and-white answers. If our hearts are submitted, however, we will be seeking to find a way to obey our authorities if there is a way to be found. And the Lord then will undoubtedly lead us through these challenging life choices. Throughout this chapter, we will study the guidelines and examples in God's Word that will aid us in handling these matters in a submissive manner.

Please keep in mind, however, that we are living in a day and age in which the crisis is *not* misuse of authority. Rather, this age is infected with the spirit of independence and rebellion. Look at 2 Timothy 3:1–5:

> But know this, that in the last days perilous times will
> come: For men will be lovers of themselves, lovers of
> money, boasters, proud, blasphemers, disobedient to
> parents, unthankful, unholy, unloving, unforgiving,

slanderers, without self-control, brutal, despisers of good, traitors, headstrong, haughty, lovers of pleasure rather than lovers of God, having a form of godliness but denying its power. And from such people turn away!

Most of these descriptions are rooted in unbrokenness and rebellion. We must go against the spirit of today in order to follow Christ in submission. And now as we look at these exceptions throughout this chapter, please keep in mind that's what they are—exceptions.

IN THE MIDST OF TURMOIL

We *can* come to the point at which we can't handle the pressure we experience under our authority. I know people who are convinced no matter what, we should suffer under their decisions, without voicing concerns or asking any questions. However, if we make sure our hearts are right and there is no bitterness or rebellion in them toward our authority, it is proper that we go to them when there is a concern or confusion.

Several times during David's run for his life, he basically responds to the situation saying, "As far as I know my heart is right. So why do you seek to kill me? If I have done something wrong, please tell me."[1] It is obvious that he did not speak out of a rebellious heart, but rather a submissive one. This is true even though he questioned the actions of his authority. Great care should be taken, however, in these situations that we act in a spirit of humility and submission of our Lord Jesus and not in the spirit of pride and accusation of Satan.

The Lord understands and knows our hearts. Difficult circumstances under our authorities may bring us to the place of an emotional, mental or physical breakdown, such that we may need to consider removing ourselves from under our authority. This may not have as much to do with our authority's sin and failure as it does with *our own* lack of maturity.

We may be able to carry 100 kilograms on our head, but cannot handle when 200 kilograms are placed on us. We will break our neck and our back if we don't get out of that situation. But it is important that we always seek the Lord. He knows how much we are able to handle, and more often than not, this amount is greater than we realize.

This could be exactly what happened with John Mark, the young man who joined Paul's aggressive missions team.[2] For whatever the reason he quit the journey, he was obviously no longer able to continue. John Mark appears *not* to have left out of rebellion or bitterness because he continued in the work of God to the extent that Paul later wrote to Timothy, "Get Mark and bring him with you, because he is helpful to me" (2 Timothy 4:11, NIV).

Just because we speak with our authorities about difficulties or choose to remove ourselves from under their authority does not automatically mean we are rebellious. Again, submission and rebellion are a matter of the heart. We sin in our actions only if we leave with rebellion in our hearts and words of attack toward authorities on our tongues.

WHEN LEAVING IS THE OPTION

There are some situations in which leaving and releasing ourselves from our authority is the best option.

It may be that we have a particular conviction about something that varies from our authority's. That difference can wear us down to the extent that it is best for us to choose to leave a ministry or employment.

I know of a man named Greg who once worked with a ministry. At that time, they were smuggling Bibles into the closed countries of Eastern Europe. For him, this became a serious issue. He told his leaders that he could not be part of a group involved in smuggling. They tried to help him see why they chose this action over leaving these people without the Word of God. He was not satisfied. In the end, he chose to leave. It took him several years before he began seeing things in a different light and understood the heart of this mission.

Throughout his struggles, Greg never attacked or criticized his leaders or their ministry. His was a godly example of someone removing himself from under authority when the conflict was greater than what he was able to handle.

A pastor friend of mine told me the story of an attractive godly wife and mother. Her name was Susan. She gave her life to Christ as a young girl. She hoped to marry a Christian young man and to have children who walked close to the Lord. While in college, she met that man. Tom was everything she was looking for. Soon they were happily married.

As the years rolled by, Tom changed. He was no longer the faithful husband Susan had once known. Getting drunk and coming home late became the norm. Often Susan cried herself to sleep.

Things got worse. From time to time, Tom visited prostitutes. Susan was heartbroken. She talked to him about her deep concern for him and this dangerous road he was on. Tom just hardened his heart and rebuked her for not being a submissive wife.

Over time, Tom's behavior went from bad to worse. One day, out of desperation, Susan called my friend Pastor Joshua and asked if he could talk to the two of them. He agreed. My friend was shocked when Tom confessed that he had been living a wilder life than even his wife had known. After several counseling sessions, my friend thought there was a sincere breakthrough. Tom seemed to be freed from his wayward lifestyle.

One day, however, Susan called Pastor Joshua and told him the nightmare was not yet over. In the midst of all her pain and trauma, she remained faithful to Tom the best she knew how. She loved him, prayed for him and even covered for him before her observant children. Often, though, he accused her of judging him.

Eventually Susan came to the place of becoming deeply concerned for the physical safety of her family. She began wondering if she should leave Tom for their sake. This is when Pastor Joshua called me once again.

When it comes to problems like this, there is no "one answer" that works every time. We must seek to know the Lord's direction for our given circumstance. God knows our hearts and the heart of our authority. He also knows what we must do within the context of the whole situation. As we seek the Lord, we must make sure that our hearts are not defiled by rebellion and that we truly want to honor Him by our decision.

When safety is at risk, it is definitely a time to consider leaving. David at last removed himself from the presence of Saul; otherwise he would have been killed.[3] Yet David did not manifest rebellion toward Saul. If we sincerely seek to honor the Lord and submit, He will work things out in the end, even if later we wonder if we made the right choice.

My friend Pastor Joshua asked for my advice. In this particular situation, I told him I felt Susan should be open to the option of leaving.

When a battered wife comes to the church leadership seeking help, it is a mistake to just tell her to "go and submit to your husband." To do so is to add injustice to injustice or abuse to abuse. If it is a life-threatening situation, a woman needs more than a few Bible verses and superficial advice. The same is true for children who suffer from physical abuse. As the Body of Christ, we have a responsibility to intervene on behalf of people who are in desperate need of practical help.

In whatever way excruciating difficulty under authority manifests itself, it takes humility to admit it is beyond us to continue on. There is no denying that Hagar, David and Joseph are examples of those who endured much under unjust authority. They trusted in God, and in the end, they reaped great blessings for their submission in the midst of hardship. However, there is a place for recognizing our situation is more than what we are able to handle.

DISOBEYING MAN TO OBEY GOD

In the book of 1 Kings, we read the strange story of a godly young prophet.[4] The Lord had specifically instructed him to go and give a certain message to the backslidden king of Israel and to return home a different way without eating or drinking anything.

After telling King Jeroboam what God wanted said, the prophet began to leave. The king pleaded with him to have some food before he left. But he responded wisely, "Even if you were to give me half your possessions, I would not go with you, nor would I eat bread or drink water here" (1 Kings 13:8, NIV).

On the way back to Judah, an older, more seasoned prophet invited him to his home for dinner. Again the young prophet said, "No. I cannot. God told me not to." Then the old prophet falsely told him, "But God asked me to invite you to eat with me."

Hungry and tired, the young man submitted and shared a meal with this fellow servant of the Lord. Obviously this young man must have been in awe to be asked to go to the home of a seasoned man of God. Surely he looked up to him as a greater authority in representing God, as he disregarded the words already spoken to him. After the meal was over, the young prophet took off again, and soon a lion came out of the woods and mauled him.

He should *not* have listened to the older prophet, even though he represented authority in terms of age or experience. Why? This young prophet already knew what God had told him. So it is with us today. When we know beyond doubt that God has shown us what needs to be done, we must give priority to that word above others' opinion or counsel.

In our decisions to follow Christ, sometimes our own family can become a hindrance. Jesus Himself faced this temptation in His earthly life. Listen to what our Lord said about this critical decision: "If anyone comes to me and does not hate his father and mother, his wife and children, his brothers and sisters—yes, even his own life—he cannot be my disciple" (Luke 14:26, NIV).

Well-meaning parents can demand that you marry a certain

person or take up a particular profession they think is the best for you and your family. It is wise to take counsel from your parents even when they are no longer responsible for you. They know you better than most people and have lived longer. *But* there may be times when God has made clear to you the path you must take, and this call of God on your life is different from their wishes. The question then before you is, Whose voice will you obey?

First, we need to make sure we are sincerely seeking to hear the Lord and not just what we want to hear. If there is no doubt that this is God's plan and not your own, then in humility you must ask your parents to please understand what you have heard from God, and pray for Him to work on their hearts. But in the end, you may have to say no to them, in order to say yes to your Lord.

This situation can happen in regard to full-time Christian service, even when your parents are believers. They insist that their children not go in some direction. Maybe they want their family business carried on. These are very difficult situations. But again, this would be a time when you must choose to follow the call of God on your life rather than obeying your human authority.

When Jesus called John and his brother, they immediately left their father's fishing business and followed Him.[5] Paul said that when God called him to preach to the Gentiles, he did not consult with his flesh and blood.[6]

During the early 1970s, I had a young man on the same missions team I was on who had to make a painful choice between the Lord Jesus and his parents.

While studying at the university, he had given his life to Christ. His family, however, was extremely anti-Christian. Yet, full of faith, he excitedly told his parents about his choice to follow Jesus.

First they were in shock. They tried their best to get him to change his mind. Then they demanded that he deny Christ and return to the religion of his ancestors. They even began to physically and mentally torture him. Though he knew he would lose his privilege of being considered their son, he stood firm in his faith. Finally they threw him out of their home. He joined our missions team, and it became my responsibility to protect him from those who sought to kidnap him and do him harm.

When the apostles and early Christians were asked not to talk about Christ, they responded to the ruling authorities, "Judge for yourselves whether it is right in God's sight to obey you rather than God. For we cannot help speaking about what we have seen and heard" (Acts 4:19–20, NIV).

Watchman Nee of China, a devout follower of Jesus, spent years in prison for disobeying the governmental authority that told him not to preach the Gospel. They demanded that he deny Christ, but he refused.

We are told to search the Scriptures and to be on the alert so we will not fall under judgment.[7] More simply stated, when our authority asks us to walk contrary to the Word of God, we must not simply obey and blindly follow.

But be careful, this is tricky ground. We should realize there is not a single person who is perfect, and that includes the delegated authorities over us. Nor do we ourselves have all the divine wisdom. We can't count on the premise that we have interpreted all Scripture accurately while others have failed. With humility, we must seek the Lord in these cases and ask Him to show us how we are to respond.

Consider Joseph's steward.[8] He was asked by Joseph, his authority, to put his silver cup in Benjamin's grain sack. Then the next day he was told to go after these men and accuse them of the very thing he himself did. It would have been easy for him to have said, "Joseph, what you are doing is wrong, and I will have no part in it." But there was a much bigger picture than what the steward understood. Joseph's brothers had shown rash jealousy toward him, and Joseph wanted to know if they still felt this way and whether they would treat his younger brother, Benjamin, in the same manner they had treated him. Of course, the steward did not know this background or how Joseph intended to handle events as they unfolded.

Often we may know only a small part of the story that our authority is dealing with. So to us it may look obviously wrong, but if we knew everything going on, we might feel quite differently. What is the answer then? We must walk with the knowledge of the Scriptures *and* the counsel of the Holy Spirit, seeking to honor and submit to our authority.

Look at the children of Israel in ancient Egypt.[9] They prospered until a new Pharaoh came into power who did not know Joseph. This new ruler feared the strength of the children of Israel and decided to oppress them. He commanded the midwives to kill all Hebrew male children at birth: "When you help the Hebrew women in childbirth and observe them on the delivery stool, if it is a boy, kill him; but if it is a girl, let her live" (Exodus 1:16, NIV). But the midwives feared God more than they did Pharaoh and *did not* obey the order. They let the boy babies live.

Moses' parents also *disobeyed* Pharaoh's order. They hid Moses and, by doing so, saved his life. Both the midwives and the parents of Moses chose to disobey the ruler's command and instead to obey God.

There may come a time in our lives when we cannot obey man for the sake of obeying God. Let us be ready to do so if we must.

IN THE SPIRIT OF HUMILITY

When we disobey delegated authority, we should do so in a spirit of humility. It is possible to be "righteous" but with a spirit of self-righteousness, which God hates. We can have all the right reasons yet be full of pride and arrogance. God wants us to do His will undefiled by the spirit of Lucifer.

The prophet Daniel is a perfect example of disobeying with a spirit of humility, not rebellion. He and his three friends were captives in Babylon in the service of the king. There was a certain amount of changing that the Babylonian authorities deemed necessary for their service—their diet, their language and their names.[10]

The diet the king ordered for them was to aid in their service in the palace. But by eating these foods, they would violate their obedience to God. So we read, "Daniel purposed in his heart that he would not defile himself with the portion of the king's delicacies, nor with the wine which he drank" (Daniel 1:8). So Daniel and his friends chose to disobey the king's order. But there was no trace of rebellion in their attitude. How did they do it?

They did not say, "What on earth is wrong with you, Babylonians? Don't you know that *we* are people who fear the living God, the God of Israel? You cannot ask us to do this! We won't participate in this sin. No way." This was *not* their attitude. They simply said to the king's eunuch, "Would you please allow us just 10 days of eating our own simple diet, and you can watch and see how we look and fare? We will do whatever you say" (Daniel 1:11–13, paraphrased).

We can become trapped into disobeying our authority, thinking it is right because of our culture, our convenience or our hidden motives. Yet as you witness these young men's attitude toward authority and the way they made their appeal in humility, it is obvious they were sincere. I imagine they folded their hands, bowed their heads and pleaded. Whatever they did, it brought them favor. And you know what God did? God made it up to them. When the test was over, they were stronger and more able than all the others, and the case was closed.

Soon there came another, even more severe test for these three friends of Daniel.[11] King Nebuchadnezzar, overcome by his own importance, decided to make an image of gold, as tall as an eight-story building. On the day of dedication, everyone was commanded to bow down and worship his statue. The penalty for refusal was to be cast into a fiery furnace!

These three young Hebrews decided not to obey the command. When the king heard of their refusal, he was furious. How dare they disobey his order? Their response was: "If we are thrown into the blazing furnace, the God we serve is able to save us from it, and he will rescue us from your hand, O king. But even if he does not, we want you to know, O king, that we will not serve your gods or worship the image of gold you have set up" (Daniel 3:17–18, NIV).

The king was livid. He ordered the furnace to be made seven times hotter than usual. Then the three were thrown into it. The flames were so intense they killed the soldiers who carried out the order. Yet when these godly young men came out, their clothing was not burned, and their bodies were not scorched.

Notice that during this entire trial, they maintained themselves in a spirit of humility. There was *no* sign of rebellion in their voices. They answered the king with respectful words. When they were proven right, their attitude was not one of pride or arrogance. There was no condemnation, no accusation or reproach against their authority.

Meanwhile, Daniel continued to be faithful, and at age 90, he was a powerful figure in the new nation of Persia.[12] Because of his elevated position, there were those who were jealous of him. They sought a reason to get rid of Daniel but could find no fault in his character or conduct.

Then they realized they could trap him by his submission to the living God. The king at the time, King Darius, was lured by his administrators to make a law that no one was allowed to pray to any other deity except the king. All who disobeyed would be thrown to the lions. Daniel chose to disobey, and that's eventually where he ended up.

Yet God shut the mouths of the lions, and Daniel was safe. Take note: Daniel chose to disobey his delegated authority, *but* with a spirit of humility. Listen to his words to his earthly king: " 'O king, live forever! My God sent his angel, and he shut the mouths of the lions. They have not hurt me, because I was found innocent in his sight. Nor have I ever done any wrong before you, O king' " (Daniel 6:21–22, NIV). As Daniel addressed the king, there was *no* sense of reproach or accusation.

Before, during and after this trial, Daniel maintained a gentle spirit, willing to suffer for the sake of submission to the living God.

PRICE TO PAY

If we do disobey, we *must* make absolutely certain that the delegated authority is acting in violation of God's Word and that the Lord desires us to oppose our authority in this particular situation. But then, once we know, we must be willing to suffer for the privilege of having done what is right—obeying God.

A few years ago, a letter came to me from one of my radio listeners in India. He had been transferred to a new city where the norm was to take bribes. Even his authorities did. At the end of the month, they divided the loot equally among all of them. Being a follower of Christ, he refused to join in their wrongdoing. Week after week, he faced opposition and ridicule. Finally, they cooked up a case against this man, telling his higher authorities that *he* took bribes. Because of this, he lost his job. I still remember his statement: "I am sad that I lost my job, but I am happy that I pleased the Lord."

In Hebrews 11, we read about those God proclaimed to be heroes of faith—men and women who made a significant mark in history by their righteousness. They were sawn asunder, brutally abused and murdered. Their rights were violated, and they were killed. Many of them had to say to a delegated authority,

"We can't obey you. We must obey God." They paid the price with their very lives.

The suffering in the early Church is the story of many who chose to disobey human authorities, knowing they may have to face martyrdom. The pages of history are stained with the blood of the martyrs, who refused to deny Christ and the Word of God.

Tens of thousands became the heroes of the catacombs. In ancient Rome, the emperor introduced "Caesar worship." Every citizen was commanded to take a pinch of incense, put it on a Roman altar once a year and say "Caesar is Lord." Punishment for not obeying was a cruel death.

Dietrich Bonhoeffer, a devout follower of Christ and a Church leader, suffered much for refusing to submit to the sinful schemes of Adolf Hitler. Bonhoeffer in humility resisted Hitler's regime for the sake of remaining loyal to God. In the end he too died as a martyr.

I remember a letter that came to us from Burma, written by one of the sisters there. A couple of our missionaries went to the mission field to this particular village. They were in a hostile Buddhist community, and yet they planted a small church. One dear sister there gave her life to the Lord, but her husband turned against her. Then the village chief and the whole community turned against the handful of believers in the village. This sister wrote the following words:

"All I needed to do was to deny Christ. My husband would have been happy. He gave me a choice: Either deny Christ or leave." She wept and pleaded, but he wouldn't change.

Meanwhile, the problems became more severe because the

village chief said, "There is no way you people can be Christians in my community. You must deny Christ or leave."

The sister's letter continued, "I took my little baby girl and whatever I could carry. I walked away with a handful of other believers, and my prayer is that someday my husband will come to know Jesus the way I know Him." Then she added, "I am praying and hoping that my little girl will grow up, become a missionary and go back to her village to share the love of God."

Peter tells us that if we suffer for doing evil there is no glory in it, but if we do what is right and then suffer for it, we are to rejoice because it is our privilege.[13] Refusing to obey an ungodly authority when we must and instead submit to God often means we must suffer.

If you come to an incident in your life in which you have to disobey your authority, may you be like Daniel. May your actions be done in the spirit of Christ, not that of Lucifer.

Let us be so sensitive that we stop when we feel our hearts are being defiled by the spirit of rebellion. Instead, make sure you know with a clear conscience that your choice to disobey is based on godliness and not on your flesh. Even when resistance is the obvious right choice, it takes humility to disobey authority in a way that pleases the Lord.

It is my prayer that the decisions you and I make to follow the Lord will not be based on time, but on eternity. Not many decades will pass before we are gone from this earth. All that we will be in eternity is determined by the choices we make right now. I pray that God in His grace will take us further into understanding the ways of God and godliness.

*L*ord, thank You for Your mercy, for Your goodness and Your longsuffering with each one of us. You remain our heavenly Father, and we are Your sons and daughters. Thank You for such encouragement and confidence because of Your love. We trust You, Lord, to help us execute decisions that are sometimes difficult and painful. Your grace is sufficient. Continue, O Lord, to deliver us from the spirit of Lucifer, that our lives may be marked by the spirit of the Lamb of God. Shower us with Your grace and Your strength. Amen.

Study Guide for Chapter 10 begins on page 252.

PRAYER

Dear Lord Jesus,

We are painfully aware of our need for Your grace to help us understand the hardness of our hearts—hardened by our pride and self-centeredness. Please create in us a thirst that will overcome all fears that keep us from an all-out surrender to Your will. Deliver us from the urge to fight for our rights, prestige, power and position. Help us to know that being under Your yoke is the way for us to know You intimately and to touch godliness.

The spirit of Lucifer has so often deceived us to rebel against You and Your authority over us. We acknowledge with true repentance that we have hurt You and made You sad by our thoughts and actions. Satan, our flesh and the world have blinded our eyes from seeing Your eternal purpose through our life of submission. We are truly sorry for our sin of rebellion and repent of it.

Please help us comprehend the blessedness of being Your lambs. Remind us so we never forget: When we are called to suffer, we are given the privilege to enter into Your suffering and thus become more like You in Your humility and lowliness.

Lord, we choose to trust You so completely with our future. Our earnest desire is to honor You above the opinions of others, our feelings and our ambitions.

May we live in total obedience and submission as You lived before Your Father. Amen.

If this book has been a blessing,

I would really like to hear from you.

Please send me an email at kp@gfa.org.

Notes

FRONT MATTER

1. C.S. Lewis, *The Weight of Glory: And Other Addresses* (New York: HarperSanFrancisco, 2001), p. 170.

INTRODUCTION

1. See John 10:10.
2. See Job 42:1–6.
3. See John 1:29.
4. Revelation 7:17, NLT.

CHAPTER 1: THE CORE OF SUBMISSION

1. 2 Corinthians 1:19.
2. See John 10:10, NIV.
3. See Genesis 2:9, 2:17.
4. See Romans 5:12–14.
5. Charles R. Swindoll, *Strengthening Your Grip: Essentials in an Aimless World* (Waco, TX: Word Books, 1982), pp. 242–243.
6. A.W. Tozer, *The Pursuit of God* (Camp Hill, PA: Christian Publications, Inc., 1982), p. 102.
7. Exodus 3:14.
8. Major W. Ian Thomas, *The Saving Life of Christ* and *The Mystery of Godliness* (Grand Rapids, MI: Zondervan Publishing House, 1988), p. 190.

9. Genesis 1:3.
10. Watchman Nee, *Spiritual Authority* (New York: Christian Fellowship Publishers, Inc., 1972), p. 22.
11. Exodus 5:2, paraphrased.
12. Isaiah 9:6.
13. See Philippians 2:7–8.
14. See Philippians 2:8.
15. See Jude 1:8–10.
16. See Romans 1:5–6.
17. See Deuteronomy 21:18–21.
18. See Numbers 16:1–33.
19. See 1 Samuel 15:1–35; 1 Kings 22:1–40.
20. Paul E. Billheimer, *Destined for the Throne* (Minneapolis, MN: Bethany House Publishers, 1975).
21. See 2 Corinthians 4:4.

CHAPTER 2: THE SPIRIT OF SUBMISSION

1. Paul Oakley, "Jesus Lover of My Soul (It's All about You)" Copyright © 1995 Thankyou Music (PRS) (adm. worldwide by EMI CMG Publishing excluding Europe which is adm. by kingswaysongs.com). International Copyright Secured. All Rights Reserved. Used by Permission.
2. See Genesis 1:27; Colossians 1:16.
3. See Isaiah 43:10; Romans 13:1.

4. See Matthew 28:18, KJV.

5. See Jeremiah 18:1–6.

6. See Romans 12:1.

7. See Romans 13:1–2.

8. See Luke 2:51.

9. See John 5:19, 6:38–40, 7:16–17; 1 Corinthians 15:28.

10. See 2 Kings 2:1–14.

11. See Genesis 16:9.

CHAPTER 3: THE BENEFITS OF SUBMISSION

1. See Luke 15:11–32.

2. Luke 15:18–19, paraphrased.

3. Tozer, *The Pursuit of God,* p. 100.

4. See 2 Kings 25:1–2; Jeremiah 21:7.

5. See Genesis 12:4, 13:2–13, 19:1–38.

6. See 2 Kings 5:15–27.

7. See 2 Kings 5:14.

8. See Philemon 1:8–21.

9. Philemon 1:12–13, paraphrased.

10. See Ephesians 6:1–3.

11. See Matthew 11:29.

12. See Genesis 29:1–27.

13. Numbers 11:28, KJV.

14. See Numbers 27:18–23; Deuteronomy 31:1–7.

15. See Isaiah 57:15.

16. See Luke 15:22–24.

17. See Deuteronomy 1:29–40, 6:10–25, 7:12–24, 11:8–32, 27:15–26, 28:1–68, 29:14–29, 30:1–20.

18. See Proverbs 4:10–13, 13:1, 13:13, 13:18, 15:31, 15:33, 16:20, 19:20, 22:4, 22:17–21.

19. See Ruth 1:1–18, 2:2, 2:22, 3:1–18, 4:15–22.

20. Ruth 1:11–13, paraphrased.

21. Lucy Ann Bennett, "I Am the Lord's." Public domain.

CHAPTER 4: CHRIST, OUR EXAMPLE

1. Roy Hession, *The Calvary Road* (Fort Washington, PA: CLC Publications, 1990), pp. 93–94.

2. John 1:29, 1:36; 1 Peter 1:19, NLT.

3. See Romans 5:12; 1 Corinthians 15:45.

4. John 1:14.

5. See Hebrews 6:20.

6. Philippians 2:7, NASB.

7. See Hebrews 4:15.

8. 2 Peter 1:4.

9. See Genesis 1:26.

10. See Ephesians 1:4, 1:7, 1:10–11, 1:13, 3:12.

11. Matthew 11:28–29.

12. Tozer, *The Pursuit of God,* p. 64.

13. See Hebrews 5:8.

14. Matthew 11:29.

15. Jeanne Guyon, *Spiritual Torrents* (n.p.: The SeedSowers Christian Books Publishing House, [1989]), pp. 85–86.

16. See Hebrews 5:8.

17. See Luke 2:41–51.

18. See Leviticus 12:8.

19. See Matthew 13:55; Mark 6:3.

20. John 8:28.

21. John 12:50, NLT.

22. John 14:31, NASB.

23. See Luke 6:12–13.

24. See John 2:24.

25. See John 11:1–44.

26. See John 11:5.

27. See Mark 1:22.

28. See Mark 4:39; Luke 8:24, 8:26–33; John 11:43–44.

29. Watchman Nee, *Secrets to Spiritual Power,* comp., Sentinel Kulp (New Kensington, PA: Whitaker House, 1998), p. 287.

30. Nee, *Spiritual Authority,* p. 14.

31. Hession, *The Calvary Road,* p. 94.

CHAPTER 5: WE MUST OBEY DELEGATED AUTHORITY

1. Native Indian garments consisting of a long collarless shirt worn over drawstring pants.
2. There are exceptional cases where we must oppose our delegated authorities in order to obey God. See Chapter 10.
3. *Ibid.*
4. 1 Samuel 8:7, paraphrased.
5. See Numbers 30:3–15.
6. See Exodus 2:1–8; Numbers 12:1–15.
7. Numbers 12:4.
8. See Numbers 12:10.
9. See Numbers 16:1–33.
10. Numbers 16:20–21, paraphrased.
11. Numbers 16:23–24, paraphrased.
12. See Leviticus 10:1–2.
13. See Exodus 6:23, 24:1, 24:9, 28:1; Leviticus 10:1; Numbers 3:2, 3:4, 26:60–61; 1 Chronicles 6:3, 24:1–2.
14. See Leviticus 10:1–2; Numbers 3:4, 26:61.
15. Matthew 6:9–10; Luke 11:2.
16. Matthew 6:13; Luke 11:4.
17. See Ephesians 2:2.
18. See Genesis 9:20–29.
19. C.S. Lewis, *The Lion, the Witch and the Wardrobe* (New York: Harper Trophy, 1978), pp. 40–41, 121–132.
20. See 2 Samuel 15:1–15, 15:30–31, 16:15–17:15, 17:21–23, 18:9–15.
21. See 2 Samuel 16:23.
22. See 2 Samuel 11, 23:34.
23. See 2 Samuel 12:13.
24. Stephen R. Covey, *The Seven Habits of Highly Effective People: Restoring the Character Ethic* (New York: Simon & Schuster, 1989), pp. 81–88.
25. See Proverbs 13:18.
26. Isaiah 45:1.
27. See Acts 9:26–30, 11:19–30, 12:25–13:13, 13:42–51, 15:36–41.
28. See Acts 9:26–27.
29. See Acts 11:25–26, 13:2, 13:7.
30. See Acts 13:43.
31. See Colossians 4:10, KJV.
32. 2 Timothy 4:11.
33. Numbers 13:27.
34. See Numbers 13:26–33.
35. Numbers 14:2, NIV.
36. See Numbers 14:13–25.
37. See Numbers 14:34–38.

CHAPTER 6: OUR RESPONSE TO AUTHORITY

1. See Genesis 4:1–15.
2. See Genesis 8:15–11:32.
3. See Exodus 20:1–17.
4. See 1 Timothy 5:17.
5. See Ephesians 5:23.
6. See Acts 20:28–29; 1 Peter 5:2–4.
7. See Acts 15:13–22.
8. See Genesis 2:18–25.
9. See Ephesians 5:33; Colossians 3:18.
10. Dr. Emerson Eggerichs, *Love & Respect* (Nashville, TN: Thomas Nelson, Inc., 2004), p. 4.
11. Ideas taken from Eggerichs, *Love & Respect*, pp. 14–15.
12. Matthew 12:48.
13. John 2:4, KJV.
14. See 2 Samuel 15:1–12.
15. A loincloth worn by some men in India.
16. See Romans 13:7.

CHAPTER 7: GODLY EXAMPLES OF SUBMISSION

1. See Matthew 4:4.
2. See Acts 9:1–30, 11:19–26, 13:1–3, 13:42–44, 14:3, 14:27–28, 15:6–29, 16:16-34, 18:12–15, 19:10, 21:30–40, 22:22–30, 23:1–35, 24:1–25:27, 27:3, 27:42, 28:30–31; Galatians 1:1, 1:18.
3. See Philippians 3:5–6.
4. Acts 9:4–5.
5. Acts 9:5.
6. Acts 9:5.
7. Acts 9:6.
8. Acts 9:6.
9. See Acts 13:42–44, 14:3, 14:27–28, 19:10, 28:30–31.
10. See Galatians 1:18.
11. See Acts 19:35–41, 21:26–36, 21:37–40, 22:22–29, 23:7–35, 27:3, 27:42–43, 28:30–31.
12. Acts 18:14–15, paraphrased.
13. Acts 23:4.
14. Acts 23:5.
15. See 1 Samuel 13:8–14, 16:1–19:18, 20:1–7, 22:1–5, 23:14–29, 24:1–22, 26:1–25; 2 Samuel 1:1–27, 2:1–7, 5:1–4, 7:1–17; 1 Chronicles 11:9.
16. 1 Samuel 16:1, paraphrased.
17. See 1 Samuel 18:17, 18:25.
18. 1 Samuel 22:5, NIV.
19. See 1 Samuel 24:4, 24:10.
20. 1 Samuel 24:8.
21. 1 Samuel 24:9–14, paraphrased.
22. 1 Samuel 24:16, NIV.
23. 1 Samuel 24:17, 24:19, NIV.
24. See Psalm 27:13.
25. 2 Samuel 1:13, NIV.
26. 2 Samuel 1:13, NIV.
27. 2 Samuel 1:15.
28. 2 Samuel 2:1, NIV.
29. See 2 Samuel 5:4.
30. See 1 Chronicles 11:9.
31. See 1 Chronicles 14:17.
32. See Genesis 37:2–36, 39:1–23, 40:15, 41:1–7, 41:38–57, 42:1–24, 43:1–34, 45:1–8, 46:28–34, 47:1–12, 49:22–24, 50:15–21.
33. Genesis 37:10, paraphrased.
34. Genesis 37:14, paraphrased.
35. Genesis 37:13.
36. Genesis 37:19, NIV.
37. Genesis 37:20, NIV.
38. See Genesis 42:21.
39. See Genesis 37:2, 41:46.
40. Genesis 41:55, NLT.
41. See Genesis 43:7.
42. See Matthew 16:25.
43. See Isaiah 57:15.
44. See Genesis 39:2–3, 39:5, 39:21–23, 45:8; 1 Samuel 18:14; 2 Samuel 5:10, 8:14; 1 Chronicles 14:17; Acts 13:42–44, 14:3, 14:27–28, 19:10–11.

CHAPTER 8: WHY WE REBEL

1. See Genesis 3:17.
2. See Isaiah 14:12–15.
3. See Psalm 40:7–8; John 10:18.
4. Nee, *Spiritual Authority,* p. 99.
5. Genesis 3:1–5, paraphrased.
6. Nee, *Spiritual Authority,* p. 21.
7. See Romans 8:7.
8. See 2 Kings 5:1–14.
9. See 2 Kings 5:12.
10. See Isaiah 14:12–15.
11. See Isaiah 14:13–14.
12. William Ernest Henley, "Invictus," in *Modern British Poetry,* ed., Louis Untermeyer (New York: Harcourt, Brace and Howe, Inc., 1920), p. 10. Public domain.
13. See Luke 15:11–32.
14. Luke 15:29–30, paraphrased.

15. See Psalm 78.
16. See Revelation 12:3–4.
17. See Numbers 16:1–40.
18. See Numbers 13:31–14:4.
19. See Romans 16:17; 1 Corinthians 5:11; 2 Timothy 3:1–5.
20. Genesis 6:22, NIV.
21. See Deuteronomy 32:39; 2 Chronicles 20:6; Job 42:2.
22. See Exodus 33:19, 34:6–7; Psalm 31:19; Psalm 34:8.
23. See Genesis 16:9–10.
24. See Joshua 21:45.

CHAPTER 9: BIBLICAL PRINCIPLES FOR EXERCISING AUTHORITY

1. See 2 Samuel 24.
2. See Titus 2:3–4.
3. See 1 Samuel 2:12, 2:22–36, 4:17.
4. See Daniel 4.
5. See 1 Kings 12:25–30, 15:33–34, 16:11–13; 2 Kings 13:1–7, 21:1–15.
6. Herbert Prochnow and Herbert Prochnow Jr., *5100 Quotations for Speakers and Writers* (Grand Rapids, MI: Baker Book House, 1986), p. 432.
7. Hession, *The Calvary Road*, p. 95.
8. Matthew 11:29, NASB.
9. See 2 Chronicles 26:1–21.
10. See Revelation 3:17–20.
11. See 1 Timothy 1:15.
12. C.S. Lewis, *Mere Christianity* (New York: HarperCollins Publishers, Inc., 2001), p. 128.
13. *Compact Oxford English Dictionary of Current English*, 3rd ed., s.v. "lord."
14. Definition taken from http://encarta.msn.com/encnet/features/dictionary/DictionaryResults.aspx?refid=1861605901. (Accessed April 27, 2008).

15. See 1 Peter 5:1–3.
16. Watchman Nee, *The Character Of God's Workman* (New York: Christian Fellowship Publishers, Inc., 1988), p. 163.
17. See 1 Timothy 3:1.
18. See John 13:4–15.
19. D.E. Hoste took over the leadership of the China Inland Mission after Hudson Taylor.
20. Phyllis Thompson, *D.E. Hoste* (London: China Inland Mission, n.d.), p. 217.
21. See Luke 15:11–32.
22. See Exodus 15:23–25, 16:2–12, 17:1–4.
23. See Exodus 32:7–14; Numbers 11:1–2, 14:10–20.
24. See 1 Kings 12:1–19; Matthew 23:10–12.
25. See 2 Corinthians 1:8–3:3.
26. See Numbers 12:3, KJV.
27. Numbers 20:8, paraphrased.
28. Numbers 20:12, paraphrased.
29. Copyright © 2010 DaySpring Cards and Roy Lessin. Used by permission, all rights reserved. www.dayspring.com.

CHAPTER 10: WHEN OUR AUTHORITIES GO WRONG

1. See 1 Samuel 20:8, 24:11, 26:18.
2. See Acts 12:25, 13:13.
3. See 1 Samuel 19:9–12.
4. See 1 Kings 13:1–24.
5. See Matthew 4:21–22.
6. See Galatians 1:16.
7. See Acts 17:11.
8. See Genesis 44:1–12.
9. See Exodus 1:6–2:4.
10. See Daniel 1:3–16.
11. See Daniel 3:1–27.
12. See Daniel 6:1–23.
13. See 1 Peter 2:20.

Touching
GODLINESS

Study Guide

INTRODUCTION

OVERVIEW

- Unsatisfied with superficial Christianity, many yearn for a deeper spiritual reality.

- Those who have touched godliness have an air of mystery, beauty and freshness about them—the look of "another world" in their eyes.

- Others desperately desire what these simple, devoted people have, yet they find themselves on the outside, looking in.

- The key that will unlock the door is submission.

- Jesus' life epitomized surrender and submission. And those who follow the Lamb will embrace these attitudes too.

- We live in a time that values independence, but Christ invites us to walk with Him on a different path and discover the mystery of godliness.

REFLECTION AND ACTION

1. Several attributes of godliness—for example, "a gentle spirit"—are mentioned in the Introduction. Make a list of these. Which quality do you find most desirable? Which do you find most challenging? Do you believe God can cultivate these qualities in your life? Are you willing to do what it takes to see change?

2. Read endnote 2 (Job 42:1–6) about Job's response to God. What do you see in his response that you'd like to see in your own life? Why do you think Job was able to change his response to God?

3. Are you yearning for a deeper sense of godliness in your own life? What steps have you taken in pursuit of it? What has been the result of your pursuits to date? Are you still "on the outside"? Be honest before the Lord: Do you think something could be standing in your way? If so, what do you think that is?

4. Is there something the Lord has been asking you to surrender to Him that you are still holding onto? Will you consider surrendering that to Him now in order to experience the new life that He promises?

5. Think about the events that led you to read this book. Take time to write down any needs, hopes and fears you have as you begin this study. Commit these thoughts into the care of your loving Heavenly Father and trust Him to take care of each one as you go through this study.

ONE

THE CORE OF SUBMISSION

OVERVIEW

- Everything around us operates on the principle of submission, and to the extent that submission is heeded, to the same extent that way is prospered.

- Submission is a choice toward life.

- Adam chose death, and we are born into this curse.

- Submission to God includes submission to delegated authority.*

- It is out of God's love for us that He asks us to submit.

- Authority is and flows from God Himself, and the principle of submission to authority is eternal, sacred and foundational.*

- Where is your heart? Are you fighting, or are you surrendered?

- Adam's curse is broken as we surrender and choose the way of the cross as Christ did.*

- Just as Christ manifests absolute submission and surrender, Satan manifests absolute rebellion.*

- God created us to depend on Him, and only what is done in His Spirit will last.

- Through the mystery of submission to authority, God is restoring creation back to innocence. When we submit, we become part of that work.*

   * These topics are developed more fully in later chapters.

REFLECTION AND ACTION

1. Reflect on your day. Write down some of the many different ways you saw the principle of submission to authority at work in nature, in society and in your personal life. How might your day have been different if the response in each of those cases was defying submission? What was the result of submission in each of those cases?

2. Note each time that the words "choice" or "choose" were used in this chapter. What are we choosing between? And what is the outcome of the choices made? In the Garden of Eden, what did the two trees represent? What was God's purpose in allowing Adam and Eve to choose between them? Can you recall an incident recently in which you were faced with the same kind of choice? How did you respond?

3. Prayerfully review all the Scripture passages on page 25 related to submission within the Trinity itself. How does this glimpse into the very heart of God change the way you think about submission? Meditate on Isaiah 43:10–11. How would you explain to someone else the concept of God and authority? Why is this principle so important and holy?

4. It can be painful to admit, even to ourselves, that we may imitate Lucifer, rather than Christ, in our attitude toward authority. However, by allowing God to reveal truth to us, we

are taking our first steps toward godliness. With that perspective, review the questions on pages 26–27 and ask the Lord to speak to you through them in any way He chooses.

5. What are the reasons why we find it difficult to submit to authority? And how is it possible for us to remain in rebellion for years *after* having received Jesus as our Savior? Write down specific times you can look back and see how you remained in rebellion. How would you want to handle those times now?

6. The author writes (top of page 30): "Nothing will remain in eternity that is not of the Spirit." Explain what this means to you and how it applies to your own ministry.

7. What does God want to accomplish through giving us the freedom to choose submission? Write down any changes in your thoughts and attitude toward submission as you've studied this chapter. Close your time by thanking God for His kindness to open your eyes to the things He showed you through this chapter.

The Spirit of Submission

Overview

- In spite of our natural tendency toward rebellion, we should surrender our lives to God, our Creator, and submit to Him and the delegated authorities over us for the sake of God's glory.

- It is important to take the time to understand the meaning and implications of the words related to submission.

- Submission isn't weakness, but rather allowing God to channel our strength His way.

- Submission isn't inferiority, but rather a choice we make independent of our authority's ability or character.

- Submission is active, seeking to understand and do what the authority really wants.

- To submit we must make deliberate choices, sometimes against our own wishes, and suffer in our flesh. We can't live a submitted life without a willingness to suffer.

- We submit out of love and respect to God as a deeply personal response.

Reflection and Action

1. List the differences between submission (*hupotasso*) and obedience (*hupakouo*)? As you study the list of differences, what do you find helpful about submission? What challenges you?

2. Have you been obedient without being submissive? Have you been submissive without being obedient? Consider your own examples. Would you want to handle it differently now? What do you find the distinction is between what is done out of submission and what is done out of obedience?

3. Explain the word *anah* using Hagar's life as an example (see Genesis 16). Why is "affliction" unavoidable to anyone seeking to follow Christ in submission?

4. Review the definition of submission to authority on page 36 and look up the related Scripture references (endnotes 2–7). After studying this chapter and God's Word, do you concur with this definition as God's will for you concerning submission to authority? Why or why not?

5. On the top of page 43, the author writes,

> Submission is a matter of the heart. It is learning to think sensitively, *What does my authority really want me to do? What is he actually saying?* It is seeking to understand and then doing it.

Take time to seek the Lord on this matter. Write down how you can currently apply this principle in relating to people in authority over you.

6. Ultimately, why should we choose to submit? Does that make choosing to submit any easier for you?

7. Throughout this challenging chapter, words of hope abound. What encouragement did you find in this chapter to help you keep pressing on toward godliness?

THREE

THE BENEFITS OF SUBMISSION

OVERVIEW

- To the extent that we submit, we will experience God's restoration to the life He planned for us. In the same way, to the extent we allow rebellion in our hearts, we repeat the chaos Satan has introduced into this world.

- Our delegated authorities are an "umbrella" that protects.

- They protect us from the spiritual powers of darkness.

- They steer us away from bad decisions and deception.

- Our submission brings into our lives healing and restoration in every way.

- Brokenness, taking Christ's yoke and being truly pliable in God's hands, is the only way we touch godliness. Submission is a powerful and active tool in this yielding of our lives.

- Brokenness and submission feed one another. God uses this brokenness and submission to train us for greater usefulness.

- Our submission allows His blessings to flow unhindered to us.

- We please the Lord when we choose to submit.

REFLECTION AND ACTION

1. Make a list of the benefits of submission described in this chapter. Which of these benefits have you already experienced in your life? Which benefits hadn't you thought of before?

2. We can learn a lot from the mistakes of Lot and Gehazi. Read the references given in endnotes 5–6. What was the deception that destroyed them? What simple action on their part could have prevented the tragedy?

3. Have you ever faced a similar situation, or do you know someone else who has? Who are the authorities God has put into your life to guide and protect you from such situations? Have you sought their guidance? If not, why not?

4. At the bottom of page 58, we read that "brokenness is incredibly important," and "from a scriptural perspective, it is at the foundation of all godliness." In your own words, explain what brokenness means. Why is it a benefit in our lives?

5. Have you allowed God to use the delegated authorities in your life to help you learn brokenness? Are you willing to see the difficulties as God's blessing and favor toward you? Take the time to talk to the Lord about this and work out any difficulties you have with it. What are the benefits of submitting to the Lord in this area?

6. Read the stories of the prodigal son from endnote 1 (Luke 15:11–32) and the slave Onesimus from endnote 8 (Philemon 1:8–21). What common themes related to authority and sub-

mission run through the two stories? What hope for your life can you glean from the endings of these stories?

7. Is there any benefit of submission discussed in this chapter that you sincerely wonder about—that is, whether God has actually promised it to you? God appreciates your honesty! Take time to read all the references in the endnotes related to that benefit, and ask God to show you the truth through His Word. Make the decision to believe what the Word of God says.

FOUR

CHRIST, OUR EXAMPLE

OVERVIEW

- Jesus' life here on earth is a perfect example of submission, and just as He overcame temptation, so can we as we follow the person the Lord Jesus Christ.

- We will manifest Christ's nature (God's eternal purpose for man) not by imitating His life but by allowing Christ's life to manifest through us as we depend on Him and bend under His yoke of submission regardless of the suffering in the flesh we must endure.

- When we die to pride and self and live in submission to God and our delegated authorities, we have rest from sin and the manifestations of the flesh.

- Jesus learned obedience through suffering, and He learned it progressively, one step at a time. He will train us the same way, not giving us more than we are capable of living out at the time.

- Jesus was tempted to disobey authority and not show them honor just as we are tempted, but He overcame the temptation and is our example.

- Are you living your life as the Lamb of God did, or are you living your life out of pride and self-assertion?

REFLECTION AND ACTION

1. What is the difference between *imitating* Christ's behavior and actually *manifesting* His nature? Can you think of a time when you attempted to simply imitate Christ? How did that go? How do we manifest His nature instead of imitating it?

2. In Matthew 11:28–30, Jesus invites us to come and learn from Him. What is the condition of His offer? What does the yoke represent? What will it produce in our lives? What will it cost us? Today, how do you practically "take His yoke upon you"?

3. Jesus suffered daily in many different ways in order to obey the will of His Father. How did Jesus suffer in the case of Lazarus (John 11:1–44)? Can you find other examples in the Gospels where Jesus endured inconvenience, misunderstanding or physical deprivation in order to carry out the will of His Father? Are you willing to suffer likewise in order to submit?

4. In spite of daily difficulties, Jesus enjoyed rest, and He promises the same to us. What kind of rest is He talking about? Do you want to experience that kind of rest in your life?

5. Jesus is our forerunner, and He showed us that we can live a life of submission. Do you believe that God can also help you overcome rebellion in your life? Memorize a Bible verse from this chapter that gives you confidence that you can overcome as Jesus did.

6. Read Hebrews 5:8. Had you ever considered before that Jesus had to "learn"? How can you see God's gentle hand teaching you obedience one step at a time?

7. Let the Lord search your heart and show you the areas in your life where you are serving out of pride and self-assertion. Take the time to surrender these areas to the Lord and ask Him to help you change. Write down anything the Lord speaks to your heart.

FIVE

WE MUST OBEY DELEGATED AUTHORITY

OVERVIEW

- Our delegated authorities represent God. It is not who they are that matters, but who they represent.

- So then, our response to our authorities is our response to God Himself.

- The people in authority over us have all been appointed by God. God backs up His delegated authorities with all His power (example: Korah).

- When we choose not to submit to the authority over us, we come under a curse and become enslaved to another.

- God has good plans for us, but in our impatience and rebellion, we can forfeit God's best.

- We will be helped if we focus on how best to respond to our authorities instead of focusing on our authorities' weaknesses.

- Our submission and respect toward our authorities are not dependent on them, but on the fact that God appointed them. The independent spirit of Lucifer is at work to undermine authority. However, we should fear God and not raise our voice against authority. God will never force us to submit, but there will be consequences.

REFLECTION AND ACTION

1. Find Romans 13:1–2 in your own Bible. Mark the words that are absolute in nature: words like "all," "every" or "none." What is God communicating through His choice of these words?

2. The chapter discusses several consequences that can happen to people who reject His delegated authority. List them.

3. Think back to a recent interaction you had with someone in authority over you. How would you have acted differently if you *actually saw God* standing behind your leader? What can you do to remember this imagery in the future?

4. What was Miriam and Aaron's complaint against Moses (see Numbers 12:1–15)? Who came to Moses' defense? What was God trying to teach Miriam by choosing leprosy as her punishment? Look for evidence of repentance and grace in the story. What does this story teach you about God's ways?

5. Read the story of Korah's rebellion in the Bible from endnote 9 (Numbers 16:1–33). Try to see the events in their larger context. Why did God respond so drastically to Korah's rebellion? What do you think would have been the end of the story if God had not stepped in?

6. In the middle of page 100 we read, "When others do wrong to me, they are in sin. But I am in the will of God." Explain this in your own words.

7. God's truth will remain an abstraction to us until we take steps to make it personal. Try reading this paraphrase of

Romans 13:1–2, replacing the blank with the name of one or more of your own leaders:

> Let *my* soul be subject to _____ 's authority.
> For there is no authority except from God, and
> the authorities that exist are appointed by God.
> Therefore if *I* resist _____ 's authority, *I* am
> resisting the ordinance of God.

Do not be too discouraged if your flesh kicks at these words. Every step you take toward brokenness is a victory! Finish your study by quietly sitting before your Lord and meditating on His promise that "He who has begun a good work in you will complete it until the day of Jesus Christ" (Philippians 1:6).

SIX

OUR RESPONSE TO AUTHORITY

OVERVIEW

- There are four areas of delegated authority that God has established for us: government, work, church and home.

- We should obey our civil authorities and the laws they make, pay taxes and not speak against them.

- Within our employment, we should serve our leaders as "unto the Lord," not just for reward or if our employer is kind.

- We should honor the high calling of a shepherd and heed his counsel.

- From creation, God's ordained plan is for the husband to lead and for the wife to submit. Even though their roles are different, that does not change the fact that they are spiritually equal.

- At the fall, Eve was deceived and sinned; hence, since that time, women are cursed with desiring to be in control of their husbands. Yet God asks wives to submit and respect their husbands.

- It is right and proper for children to obey their parents.

- When we sincerely submit in our hearts, there is an outward reflection of submission. Some of the ways we reflect submission are through our body language, our words, the way we listen, our appearance, wearing a head covering, humility, transparency, seeking guidance, respect for elders and loyalty.

- If you can see that you have acted in rebellion, ask for forgiveness and you will be blessed.

REFLECTION AND ACTION

1. The chapter lists four main categories of delegated authority. List people in authority over you from each category. With the Lord's help, consider how you are doing in submitting to them and respecting their leadership. What are some changes you'd like to make?

2. Although we respect our civil leaders and obey the laws of our land *for the most part,* secretly we may allow ourselves "small exceptions." Do you? How do you think you should handle those exceptions?

3. Ephesians 6:5 says that we are to serve our employers with "fear and trembling, in sincerity of heart, as to Christ." Explain this in your own words and give an example of serving an employer—possibly even your own employer—in this way.

4. What are some practical ways we can submit ourselves under our pastor?

5. In God's design, every family member plays an important role, and each one is under authority. What role has God assigned to you right now? How has God used authorities within your family to protect you? To mold your character?

6. This chapter lists ten "reflections of submission." Are there any reflections of submission in particular that brought conviction? Write them down and ask the Lord to use them in your life as indicators of transformation.

7. Near the end of the chapter is a section titled "Write That Letter." Has the Holy Spirit been convicting you of rebellion against someone in authority? If so, this would be a good time to seek his forgiveness. Don't let pride or fear stand in the way of your progress toward freedom.

SEVEN

GODLY EXAMPLES OF SUBMISSION

OVERVIEW

- Follow the godly examples of those who walked in submission given to us in Scripture.

- From the beginning of his walk with Christ, Paul trusted, as from the Lord, the authorities God put in his life.

- In the midst of strain and incredible circumstances, David respected and honored his leaders, and his blessing was great.

- Joseph faithfully submitted to the Lord and the authorities he was given, and God blessed his life and his family members' lives at the proper time.

- As these men ultimately submitted to God through their circumstances and authorities in the midst of suffering and hardship, they were prepared for all that God had for them, they truly touched godliness and they were blessed.

REFLECTION AND ACTION

1. Read in your own Bible about Paul (endnote 2), David (endnote 15) and Joseph (endnote 32). What important things do their lives have in common? What specific principles of submission to authority do you see in their lives? What are the qualities in their lives that you would like to emulate?

2. Recount all the delegated authorities Paul submitted to during his years of ministry. Were you surprised to read this concerning the great Apostle Paul? Why do you think the Holy Spirit included all these details in the biblical record?

3. What were the various ways that David showed his submission to King Saul over the years of their relationship? What "reflections of submission" from Chapter 6 do you see in him? What sustained David through so many years of being pursued by Saul?

4. How did Joseph's years in prison prepare him to be a faithful prime minister to Pharaoh for the next 43 years? How did they prepare him to receive and forgive his brothers? In the area of submission, is there anything in your life right now that the Lord may want to use as a means of preparation for the future?

5. Where do you think you are in this journey of submission? Are you willing to be tested in submission as you grow?

6. With whom do you most identify—Paul, David or Joseph? Why? What quality about this man do you most admire and want for yourself? By what process did God develop that quality in him? Are you willing to have Him do the same for you? As the Holy Spirit may lead you, write down your heart's desire and commit the matter of training into the Lord's hands.

EIGHT

WHY WE REBEL

OVERVIEW

- Despite the significance and the blessings of submission, it is still an aversion to mankind because Satan is constantly at work to stir up independence and rebellion.

- Rebellion begins in our minds. Satan appeals to our mind and human reasoning to influence us to rebel.

- Before the fall, right and wrong were in God's hands.

- At the fall, innocence died. And now each man determines for himself what is best.

- *Reason we rebel 1:* We think we know better than our authority.

- *Reason 2:* Unbrokenness and pride balk at bowing their heads to another and stand in the way of submission. Our remedy is to follow Christ's example of humility.

- *Reason 3:* Unforgiveness distorts our perception of reality, and we are thus more prone toward a critical attitude and rebellion.

- When the wrong was committed by an authority figure, it makes it more difficult for us to submit to other authorities. But God can heal and restore us from our past pain.

- *Reason 4:* Negative influences from those who speak ill of leaders can sweep us into their own rebellion. Be careful whom you listen to and reject the negative words you hear!

- *Reason 5:* Rebellion stems from a lack of faith that God is truly sovereign and can be trusted. Our submission ultimately rests on our faith in God that we will "see the goodness of the LORD in the land of the living" (Psalm 27:13).

REFLECTION AND ACTION

1. Most of us would never presume to know better than *God Himself,* yet we may sincerely believe that we know better than *His delegated authorities.* Do you see a contradiction in our logic here?

2. How do we *practically* bring "every thought into captivity to the obedience of Christ" (2 Corinthians 10:5)? Why is it important that we learn to do this?

3. How would you define pride? What is God's evaluation of pride? We are often blind to the pride in our own heart. How did God bring Naaman's pride into the light from endnote 8 (2 Kings 5:1–14)? Has God ever used delegated authority in your life in the same way? How did you respond?

4. What types of events in a person's life can lead to bitterness? How can bitter people tend to respond to authority? Think back to Chapter 7. Joseph and David *could* have become bitter over the mistreatment they received from their authorities. Why didn't they? What is the antidote to bitterness?

5. Negative influences can cause great harm. How have you been impacted by negative influences? How—whether in your own church, school or workplace—did one person's discontent with authority spread to you through influence, and perhaps how did you, maybe without even thinking about it, spread that rebellion to another? How would you handle things now? What precautions would you like to put into place to make sure that doesn't happen?

6. Reflect on various decisions made by your authorities in the past that you submitted to "against your better judgment." How many of those decisions ended up in the long run to be a blessing to you? Did any of those decisions turn out to be a total disaster? (Note: If it made you more like Christ, it was not a total disaster!)

7. Ultimately, our lack of submission can be traced back to unbelief that God is truly sovereign and can be trusted. Take the time to meditate on a Bible verse that encourages you that you can truly put your faith in God. How would this faith also help you conquer reasons 1–4?

NINE

BIBLICAL PRINCIPLES FOR EXERCISING AUTHORITY

OVERVIEW

- Being in leadership, we are responsible to God for the stewardship of the people He entrusted to us. What we do as leaders ultimately affects the people for which we're responsible.

- Regardless of the position we hold, we must continue to submit to the authorities in our lives.

- God is the Authority. All authority is appointed and directed by Him, and we, as leaders, simply represent Him, the Authority.

- As leaders representing the living God, our godliness, walk with Him and character are of utmost importance because they should properly reflect our Lord.

- Being a leader doesn't mean doing whatever you want, but choosing to die daily as you carry out God's assignments. It means working more, praying more, suffering more and choosing inconveniences.

- Jesus called Himself humble. We can only rightly represent Him if we are humble, which means depending on the Lord, being willing to ask for help and admitting our failures.

- God gave man a free will. He does not force us to do anything. And as a leader, we should never try to force people to obey by fear and manipulation or attempt to control them.

- Just as Jesus served, God wants leaders who don't act superior but who look for opportunities to serve others, especially serving those to whom they're responsible.

- Love must govern our decisions as leaders and our ways of dealing with people. That includes looking for ways to help people succeed, maintain their dignity and extend grace and freedom.

- The Lord's servant doesn't strive. It is not up to us to change people or to defend ourselves. If people rebel against us, let the Lord defend us.

- Authority should never give us the license to do what we want and misuse the position that God has given to us.

- A leader who has a submissive heart has all the traits of a godly leader.

REFLECTION AND ACTION

1. We all are in authority over someone. Who are the people whom God has entrusted to you? Now that you have a better understanding of authority, how will that help you become a better leader? How does *your* submission to authority relate to your ability to lead *them*?

2. Why is a personal walk with the Lord so essential in order to exercise godly leadership? What are specific things you'd like to do to grow in your walk with the Lord?

3. How does it bless people when a leader humbles himself and confesses his own failures to them? Is this a common practice in the world? Why or why not? Are you willing to confess your failures to those you're responsible to?

4. Jesus said, "Greater love has no one than this, than to lay down one's life for his friends" (John 15:13). What principles of godly authority are covered by that one statement?

5. What does it mean, "A leader must not strive"? How did Jesus exemplify this principle in His ministry?

6. Read the account of Moses striking the rock in the wilderness (Numbers 20:1–13). Some might argue that Moses deserved more grace. Why did God judge Moses so severely? What does this mean practically for you, as you represent God to others?

7. Thinking back on the godly leaders you've had, what qualities in their life mentioned in this chapter did you most admire? Which were most instrumental in helping you grow and succeed? Think now of your own situations as one in authority. How could you be more faithful to implement these qualities in your own life?

8. How has this chapter challenged your thinking about your authorities and why you should submit to them? How will you pray differently for your leaders, now that you see the weight of responsibility on their shoulders?

TEN

WHEN OUR AUTHORITIES GO WRONG

OVERVIEW

- There are times when authorities act in such a way that we should either express concern, remove ourselves or disobey. But we must be careful that whatever we do is done out of a heart of submission and that we're not just looking for a way out.

- When we can't handle the pressure or there is a concern or confusion, it is right to talk to our authority out of the right heart and in a humble, non-accusing way.

- Removing oneself from under another's authority may be necessary when it's a matter of conviction that we can't live with or our safety is at risk.

- Needing to speak with our leader or remove ourselves from his authority is not necessarily because our authority is at fault. It could also be a lack of immaturity on our own part.

- When it is a choice between God and man, we must choose to obey God. Be cautious, however, and know for certain that it's the Lord. Remember that we don't know the full story of what our authority knows, and seek the guidance of the Holy Spirit.

- In all these circumstances, we should respond with humility and respect toward our authority, making sure we handle them in the spirit of Christ and not in the spirit of Lucifer.

- Refusal to obey an ungodly authority for the sake of obeying God often means we will suffer.

REFLECTION AND ACTION

1. Take the time to think about which is the bigger crisis in our age: misuse of authority or rebellion against authority. With that in mind, how would that affect the way you would view difficult situations with your authorities in the future?

2. What was Daniel's secret that enabled him to disobey his authorities three different times and survive? Is his response something you see in your life right now? Would you like to?

3. If you are concerned about a decision your leader has made, what would be the right set of circumstances for talking to him about it? What should the attitude of your heart be as you talk to him? How might you bring up your concern in an honoring way? What might be dishonoring?

4. Explain three situations for which the best course of action might be to withdraw oneself from under the authority of another. Why can't there be a single rule that applies to every situation? How do you determine the best response?

5. If someone in authority over us asks us to do something that we think violates God's Word, why must we be very careful in choosing our course of action? How could our limited

perspective cause us to misjudge the situation? How do we navigate through dangerous waters like these? Have you or someone you know already experienced this?

6. If we find ourselves in a place where we must disobey authority in order to obey Christ, what can we expect will happen? How does this reality change your perspective on the authorities you have now?

7. Based on reading this chapter and going through these questions, write a list of the thoughts you'd like to keep in mind if you ever found yourself in any of the situations.

8. This sentence on the top of page 203 is a most hope-filled conclusion to our study on submission:

> If we sincerely seek to honor the Lord and submit, He will work things out in the end, even if later we wonder if we made the right choice.

What does this statement mean to you? What, then, is the best plan of action in following the Lord in submission?

9. Review your answer for question 5 from the Introduction. Write down the ways the Lord has been working in your life in the areas you listed.

GOSPEL FOR ASIA

After 2,000 years of Christianity, how can it be that nearly 3 billion people are still unreached with the Gospel? How long must they wait?

This is why Gospel for Asia exists.

More than 30 years ago, God specifically called us to invest our lives to reach the most unreached of South Asia through training and sending out national missionaries.

Gospel for Asia (GFA) is a missions organization dedicated to reaching the most unreached in the 10/40 Window. Thousands of GFA-supported pastors and missionaries serve full-time to share the love of Christ in 10 Asian countries.

National missionaries are highly effective because they work in their own or a similar culture. They already know, or can easily learn, the language, customs and culture of the people to whom they minister. They don't need visas, and they live economically at the same level as their neighbors. These advantages make them one of the fastest and most effective ways to get the Gospel to the millions who are still waiting to hear.

However, the young, economically weak Asian Church and her missionaries can't do it alone. The enormous task of reaching nearly 3 billion people takes the help of the whole Body of Christ worldwide.

That is why GFA offers those who cannot go themselves the opportunity to become senders and prayer partners of national missionaries—together fulfilling the Great Commission and sharing in the eternal harvest of souls.

To find out more information about Gospel for Asia or to receive a free copy of K.P. Yohannan's best-selling book *Revolution in World Missions,* visit our website at www.gfa.org or contact one of our offices near you.

AUSTRALIA P.O. Box 3587, Village Fair, Toowoomba QLD 4350
Phone: 1300 889 339   Email: infoaust@gfa.org

CANADA 245 King Street E, Stoney Creek, ON L8G 1L9
Toll free: 1-888-WIN-ASIA   Email: infocanada@gfa.org

FINLAND PL 165, FI-33101, Tampere
Phone: 045 359 3590   Email: infofi@gfa.org

GERMANY Postfach 13 60, 79603 Rheinfelden (Baden)
Phone: 07623 79 74 77   Email: infogermany@gfa.org

KOREA Seok-Am Blg 5th Floor, 6-9 Tereran-ro,
Yeoksam-dong, Gangnam-gu, Seoul 135-080
Toll free: (080) 801-0191   Email: infokorea@gfa.org.kr

NEW ZEALAND PO Box 302580, North Harbour 0751
Toll free: 0508-918-918   Email: infonz@gfa.org

SOUTH AFRICA P.O. Box 28880, Sunridge Park, Port Elizabeth 6008
Phone: 041 360-0198   Email: infoza@gfa.org

UNITED KINGDOM The Enterprise Centre, 6 Harper Road,
Sharston, Manchester M22 4RG
Phone: 0161 946 9484   Email: infouk@gfa.org

UNITED STATES 1800 Golden Trail Court, Carrollton, TX 75010
Toll free: 1-800-WIN-ASIA   Email: info@gfa.org